Survey of American Poetry

THE GRANGER ANTHOLOGY
SERIES II   VOLUME II

**REVOLUTIONARY ERA
1766-1799**

THE GRANGER ANTHOLOGY

Series I

THE WORLD'S BEST POETRY

Series II

THE WORLD'S BEST POETRY

Survey of American Poetry

THE GRANGER ANTHOLOGY
SERIES II   VOLUME II

REVOLUTIONARY ERA
1766-1799

**Edited by The Editorial Board,
Granger Book Company**

GRANGER BOOK CO., INC.
GREAT NECK, NEW YORK

Printed and Bound in the United States of America

CONTENTS

PREFACE

The Granger Anthology is a comprehensive conspectus of international verse in English designed to form the core of a library's poetry collection. Covering the entire range of poetic literature, *The Granger Anthology* encompasses all topics and national literatures.

Published in a multivolume continuing series format, each series is devoted to a major area of the whole undertaking, and contains complete author, title, and first line indexes. Bibliographic and biographical data is also provided.

Series I, **THE WORLD'S BEST POETRY**, with coverage through the 19th century, was recently issued in 10 volumes. The work is topically classified and arranged by subject matter. Supplement One brings the work, for English and American poetry, to 1929.

Series II, **SURVEY OF AMERICAN POETRY**, is an anthology of American verse arranged chronologically in 10 volumes. Each volume will present a significant period of American poetic history, from 1607 to 1980. Volume I, Colonial Period 1607-1765, was published in 1982.

INTRODUCTION

The revolutionary era, so rich and vital in the history of America, is not noteworthy for its poetry. Although the verse was copious, acclaimed, and influencial in its time, and included the work of the nation's first major poet, Philip Freneau, its significance lies more in its historic value than in its artistic merit.

The passage of the Stamp Act in 1765 gave rise to American nationalism and sparked an effusion of anti-British ballads. American political satire was born, and the verse was inspirational, popular, and vigorous. When this nascent nationalism began to take the shape of armed rebellion and seccession, opposing voices were raised. Loyalists to the British crown, many of whom favored constitutional rather than violent means of asserting American rights and aspirations, answered the nationalists in kind.

Poetry was then much more than now a common forum for the exposition and debate of topical issues. The satiric and often vitriolic raillieries which began with the "patriots" and the "loyalists" continued in the post-war struggle between Hamiltonians and Jeffersonians, federalists against republicans.

The new born nationalism also evoked longer, more philosophic poems which glorified America and extolled all things American. While much more ambitious and self-consciously important than the more vibrant and contentious ballads, these epic paeans were of no greater literary merit.

The period, of interest today largely because of the presence of Freneau, was mostly dominated by an antithetical group which excluded him: the "Connecticut Wits" (also variously called the "Hartford Wits" and the "Yale Poets") were highly esteemed and versatile Calvinist-federalist aristocrats who were graduates of Yale, or associated with it. Each member possessed grand literary aspirations, both personally and for the establishment of a national literature. Their accomplishments in other fields, including medicine, education, and diplomacy, however, far surpassed their literary achievements.

The end of the period, coming at the close of the century, marked the completion of the first two hundred years of native American verse. It also signaled the beginning of the phenomenal growth and development of the poetry which ensued. While the study of seventeenth and eighteenth century American verse is instructive in conveying a sense of the contemporary scene and in understanding the evolution of American institutions, it is indispensible to a full appreciation of the great poetry that was to follow.

EXPLANATORY NOTES

This anthology is arranged chronologically by date of birth of the poets so as to provide the reader with a sense of the changing nature of the verse. The dating of particular poems reprinted here presents in some cases a difficult task. When known, the date of creation (or publication) is given in parenthesis after the title in the main body.

In some cases selections from longer works are provided when such selection is deemed sufficient to convey to the general reader the essence of the work. When a selection only is reprinted, such fact is given both in the main body after the title and in the Contents. If recourse to the complete text is required, reference should be made to the collections listed in the Bibliography.

The spelling of words is repeated as they appear in the primary and secondary sources. Likewise, punctuation, capitalization, and usage has been retained. No attempt to reconcile divergent forms and usages as they may appear in the various sources has been made so that there are inconsistencies not relevant to an understanding of the material.

Authors, titles, and first lines are arranged in a single alphabetical listing in the Index. Poet names are in bold face; poem titles are in italics; and poem first lines are enclosed in quotation marks. When the title and first line are identical, only the title is given.

Survey of American Poetry

THE GRANGER ANTHOLOGY
SERIES II   VOLUME II

REVOLUTIONARY ERA
1766-1799

JUPITER HAMMOND [1720?-1800]

A New York slave, Jupiter Hammond is generally considered to be America's first published black poet. His "An Evening Thought" was issued as a broadside in 1760. His most substantial literary effort, "An Address to the Negroes in the State of New York," was published in 1787. Unlike his contemporary, Phillis Wheatley, Hammond's work evinces concern for the plight of his fellow blacks.

An Address to Miss Phillis Wheatley, selections [1778]

O come you pious youth! adore
  The wisdom of thy God,
In bringing thee from distant shore,
  To learn His holy word.

Eccles. xii.

Thou mightst been left behind,
  Amidst a dark abode;
God's tender mercy still combin'd,
  Thou hast the holy word.

Psal. cxxxv, 2, 3.

Fair wisdom's ways are paths of peace,
  And they that walk therein,
Shall reap the joys that never cease,
  And Christ shall be their king.

Psal. i. 1, 2; Prov. iii, 7.

God's tender mercy brought thee here;
  Tost o'er the raging main;
In Christian faith thou hast a share,
  Worth all the gold of Spain.

Psal. ciii, 1, 3, 4.

While thousands tossed by the sea,
  And others settled down,
God's tender mercy see thee free,
  From dangers that come down.

Death.

That thou a pattern still might be,
  To youth of Boston town,
The blessed Jesus set thee free,
  From every sinful wound.

                              2 Cor. v, 10.

The blessed Jesus, who came down,
  Unvail'd his sacred face,
To cleanse the soul of every wound,
  And give repenting grace.

                              Rom. v, 21.

That we poor sinners may obtain,
  The pardon of our sin;
Dear blessed Jesus now constrain,
  And bring us flocking in.

                         Psal. xxxiv, 6, 7, 8.

Come you, Phillis, now aspire,
  And seek the living God,
So step by step thou mayst go higher,
  Till perfect in the word.

                         Matth. vii, 7, 8.

MERCY WARREN [1728-1814]

Mercy Warren, the daughter of James Otis, colonial jurist, sister of James, revolutionary orator, and wife of James Warren, revolutionary leader, had a wide acquaintance with the public and literary men of the time.

These advantages, together with her intelligence and learning, enabled her to write the popular *History of the American Revolution* (1805), as well as several political satires in dramatic form.

Not principally a poet, her work was nonetheless well received by readers and critics, and survives today as a rare example of the work of eary American women.

Simplicity

Deep in the bosom of old Time there stood,
Just on the margin of the sea-green flood,
A virgin form, in lucid robes array'd,
Whose ebon tresses negligently play'd
In flowing ringlets, as the wavy main
Felt the soft breeze that fann'd the verdant plain;
While the young blush of innocence bespoke
Her innate worth in every graceful look;
Her meek-eyed aspect, modest and benign,
Evinced the fair one's origin divine;
Virtue, at once her ornament and shield,
And truth the trident that the goddess held,
Beneath her reign, behold a happy race,
Who ne'er contested titles, gold, or place.
Ere commerce's whiten'd sails were wafted wide,
And every bosom caught the swelling pride
Of boundless wealth, surcharged with endless snares,
Exotic follies, and destructive cares;
Ere arts, or elegance, or taste refined,
And tempting luxury assail'd mankind;
There oaks and evergreens, and poplar shades,
In native beauty, rear'd their conic heads;
The purple tinge with golden hues inwrought,
In dappled forms, as sportive nature taught;
The silken foliage open'd through the mead,
And the clear fount in wild meanders play'd;
Beside whose gentle murmuring stream there stood
The humble hamlet, by the peasant trod,
Whose heart, unblacken'd by so mean a vice,
As lust of gold, or carking avarice;
No guilty bribes his whiten'd palm possess'd,
No dark suspicion lurk'd within his breast:
Love, concord, peace, and piety and truth,
Adorn'd grey hairs and dignified the youth;
There stingless pleasures crown'd the temperate feast,
And ruddy health, a constant welcome guest,

Fill'd up the cup, and smiled at every board,
The friend and handmaid of her generous lord.
   The rosy finger'd morn, and noontide ray,
The streaked twilight or the evening gray,
Were pass'd alike in innocence and mirth,
No riot gendering slow but certain death;
Unclouded reason guided all their way,
And virtue's self sat innocently gay.
The winged hours serenly glided by,
Till golden Phœbus deck'd the western sky;
And when enwrapp'd in evening's sable vest,
And midnight shadows hush'd the world to rest,
On the famed ladder, whose extended bars,
From earth's low surface reach'd beyond the stars,
From orb to orb, thought reach'd the airy void,
Through widen'd space the busy mind employ'd,
While angel guards to watch his fate were given
Prelusive dreams anticipated heaven.
   But ere the bird of dawn had hail'd the day,
Or warbling songsters chirp'd their early lay,
The grateful heart its joyful matins raised,
And nature's God in morning anthems praised.
   Thus happy that ideal golden age,
That lives descriptive in the poet's page;
But now, alas! in dark oblivion lost,
The sons of Adam know it to their cost;
Since God forbade the mother of mankind
To taste the fruit to which she most inclined:
Her taste so delicate, refined and nice,
That the exuberance even of Paradise,
The grassy banks beside the blue cascade,
The winding streams from Pison's golden head,
The spicy groves on Gihon's lengthen'd side,
Hiddekel's fount, Assyria's blooming pride,
The fruits luxuriant on Euphrates' shores,
The rich profusion that all Eden pours,
The shady dome, the rosy vaulted bower,
And nature deck'd with every fruit and flower

Were insufficient, rude, and incomplete.
For taste ran wanton, and the fair must eat.
  Since which the garden's closely lock'd by fate,
And flaming cherubs guard the eastern gate;
This globe is traversed round from pole to pole,
And earth research'd to find so rich a dole
As happiness unmix'd:—the phantom flies,
No son of Eve has ever won the prize.
  But nearest those, who nearest nature live,
Despising all that wealth or power can give,
Or glittering grandeur, whose false optics place,
The *summum bonum* on the frailest base;
And if too near the threshold of their door,
Pride blazes high, and clamors loud for more—
More shining pomp, more elegance and zest,
In all the wild variety of taste;
Peace and contentment are refine'd away,
And worth, unblemish'd, is the villain's prey.
  Easy the toil, and simple is the task,
That yields to man all nature bids him ask;
And each improvement on the author's plan,
Adds new inquietudes to restless man.
As from simplicity he deviates,
Fancy, prolific, endless wants creates;
Creates new wishes, foreign to the soul,
Ten thousand passions all the mind control,
So fast they tread behind each other's heels,
That some new image on the fancy steals;
Ere the young embryo half its form completes,
Some new vagary the old plan defeats;
Down comes the Gothic or Corinthian pile,
And the new vista wears the Doric style.
The finer arts depopulate and waste,
And nations sink by elegance and taste:
Empires are from their lofty summits rent,
And kingdoms down to swift perdition sent,
By soft, corrupt refinements of the heart,
Wrought up to vice by each deceptive art.

Rome, the proud mistress of the world, displays
A lasting proof of what my pen essays;
High-wrought refinement—usher'd in replete,
With all the ills that sink a virtuous state;
Their sumptuary laws grown obsolete,
They, undismay'd, the patriot's frown could meet;
Their simple manners lost—their censors dead,
Spruce *petit maitres* o'er the forum tread.
I weep those days when gentle Maro sung,
And sweetest strains bedeck'd the flatterer's tongue;
When so corrupt and so refined the times,
The must could stoop to gild a tyrant's crimes.
Then paint and sculpture, elegance and song,
Were the pursuits of all the busy throng;
When silken commerce held the golden scales,
Empire was purchased at the public sales:
No longer lived the ancient Roman pride,
Her virtue sicken'd, and her glory died.
What blotted out the Carthaginian fame,
And left no traces but an empty name?—
Commerce! the source of every narrow vice,
And honor, barter'd at a trivial price.
By court intrigues, the Commonwealth's disgraced,
Both suffetes, and senators debased:
By soft refinement, and the love of gold,
Faction and strife grew emulous and bold,
Till restless Hanno urged his purpose on,
And Scipio's rival by his arts undone.
From age to age since Hannibal's hard fate,
From Cæsar's annals to the modern date,
When Brunswick's race sits on the British throne,
And George's folly stains his grandsire's crown;
When taste improved by luxury high wrought,
And fancy craves what nature never taught;
Affronted virtue mounts her native skies,
And freedom's genius lifts her bloated eyes;
As late I saw, in sable vestments stand,
The weeping fair, on Britain's naked strand.

The cloud-capt hills, the echoing woods and dales,
(Where pious Druids dress'd the hallow'd vales;
And wrote their missals on the birchen rind,
And chanted dirges with the hollow wind,)
Breathe murmuring sighs o'er that ill fated isle,
Wrapt in refinements both absurd and vile.
Proud Thames deserted—her commercial ports
Seized and possess'd by hated foreign courts;
No more the lofty ships her marts supply,
The Neriads flap their watery wings and die:
Gray Neptune rises from his oozy bed,
And shakes the sea-weed from his shaggy head;
He bids adieu to fair Britannia's shore,
The surge rebounds, and all the woodlands roar;
His course he bends toward the western main,
The frowning Titans join the swelling train,
Measure the deep, and lash the foaming sea,
In haste to hail the brave Columbia free:
Ocean rebounds, and earth reverberates,
And heaven confirms the independent states;
While time rolls on, and mightly kingdoms fail,
They, peace and freedom on their heirs entail,
Till virtue sinks, and in far distant times,
Dies in the vortex of European crimes,

JOHN DICKINSON [1732-1808]

A delegate to the Stamp Act Congress in 1765, and later a member of the Continental Congress and governor of Delaware and then Pennsylvania, Dickinson was a prolific political essayist.

He was the dominant politico-literary figure during the decade preceding the Revolution in 1775. His views coincided with and reflected the public temper of the time: strong, albeit armed, demand for the political rights of Americans, but within the context of colonialism. Being a constitutionalist rather than revolutionist, he opposed the resolution for independence in Congress in 1776.

Thus, when the public temper changed with the outbreak of hostilities to the policies favoring independence, Dickinson's adherenece to his views quickly cost him his influence. His conciliatory approach was an anachronism and antagonism and put him in disrepute.

Although he finally did support the war in fact by serving in the army against the British, he never regained the favor and acclaim he enjoyed prior to the war.

The Liberty Song [*1768*]

Come join hand in hand, brave Americans all,
And rouse your bold hearts at fair Liberty's call;
No tyrannous acts shall suppress your just claim,
Or stain with dishonor America's name.

In freedom we're born and in freedom we'll live;
   Our purses are ready,
   Steady, Friends, steady,
Not as *slaves* but as *freemen* our money we'll give.

Our worthy forefathers—let's give them a cheer—
To climates unknown did courageously steer;
Thro' oceans to deserts for freedom they came,
And dying bequeath'd us their freedom and fame.

Their generous bosoms all dangers despis'd,
So highly, so wisely, their birthrights, they priz'd:
We'll keep what they gave, we will piously keep,
Nor frustrate their toils on the land or the deep.

The Tree their own hands had to Liberty rear'd
They lived to behold growing strong and rever'd;
With transport then cried, "Now our wishes we gain,
For our children shall gather the fruits of our pain."

How sweet are the labors that freemen endure,
That they shall enjoy all the profit, secure:
No more such sweet labors Americans know,
If Britons shall reap what Americans sow.

Swarms of placemen and pensioners soon will appear,
Like locusts deforming the charms of the year:
Suns vainly will rise, showers vainly descend,
If we are to drudge for what others shall spend.

Then join hand in hand, brave Americans all;
By uniting we stand, by dividing we fall:
In so righteous a cause let us hope to succeed,
For Heaven approves of each generous deed.

All ages shall speak with amaze and applause
Of the courage we'll show in support of our laws:
To die we can bear, but to serve we disdain,
For shame is to freemen more dreadful than pain.

This bumper I crown for our sovereign's health,
And this for Britannia's glory and wealth
That wealth and that glory immortal may be,
If she is but just, and we are but free.
    In freedom we're born, &c.

FRANCIS HOPKINSON [1737-1791]

A signatory to the Declaration of Independence, Francis Hopkinson was an active and effective "word warrior" in the literary debates during the revolutionary era. Through his essays, miscellaneous writings, and verse, he established himself as the leading humorist of the day, and as an untiring champion of American independence. His most popular piece of verse, "The Battle of the Kegs" was, in his words, "occasioned by a real incident (when) certain machines, in the form of kegs, charged with gunpowder, were sent down the river to annoy the British shipping then at Philadelphia; (the British discovering the danger) manned the wharfs and shipping, and discharged their small arms and cannons at everything they saw floating in the river during ebbtide."

The Battle of the Kegs [*1778*]

Gallants attend and hear a friend,
    Trill forth harmonious ditty,
Strange things I'll tell which late befell
    In Philadelphia city.

'Twas early day, as poets say,
    Just when the sun was rising,
A soldier stood on a log of wood,
    And saw a thing surprising.

As in a maze he stood to gaze,
    The truth can't be denied, sir,
He spied a score of kegs or more
    Come floating down the tide, sir.

A sailor too in jerkin blue,
    This strange appearance viewing,
First damned his eyes, in great surprise,
    Then said, "Some mischief's brewing.

"These kegs, I'm told, the rebels hold,
    Packed up like pickling herring;
And they're come down t'attack the town,
    In this new way of ferrying."

The soldier flew, the sailor too,
    And scared almost to death, sir,
Wore out their shoes, to spread the news,
    And ran till out of breath, sir.

Now up and down throughout the town,
    Most frantic scenes were acted;
And some ran here, and others there,
    Like men almost distracted.

Some fire cried, which some denied,
   But said the earth had quaked;
And girls and boys, with hideous noise,
   Ran through the streets half naked.

Sir William, he, snug as a flea,
   Lay all this time a snoring,
Nor dreamed of harm as he lay warm,
   In bed with Mrs. L———g.

Now in a fright, he starts upright,
   Awaked by such a clatter;
He rubs both eyes, and boldly cries,
   "For God's sake, what's the matter?"

At his bed-side he then espied,
   Sir Erskine at command, sir,
Upon one foot he had one boot,
   And th' other in his hand, sir.

"Arise, arise," Sir Erskine cries,
   "The rebels—more's the pity,
Without a boat are all afloat,
   And ranged before the city.

"The motley crew, in vessels new,
   With Satan for their guide, sir,
Packed up in bags, or wooden kegs,
   Come driving down the tide, sir.

"Therefore prepare for bloody war,
   These kegs must all be routed,
Or surely we despised shall be,
   And British courage doubted."

The royal band, now ready stand,
    All ranged in dread array, sir,
With stomach stout to see it out,
    And make a bloody day, sir.

The cannons roar from shore to shore,
    The small arms make a rattle;
Since wars began I'm sure no man
    E'er saw so strange a battle.

The rebel dales, the rebel vales,
    With rebel trees surrounded;
The distant wood, the hills and floods,
    With rebel echoes sounded.

The fish below swam to and fro,
    Attacked from every quarter;
"Why sure," thought they, "the devil's to pay,
    'Mongst folks above the water."

The kegs, 'tis said, though strongly made,
    Of rebel staves ahd hoops, sir,
Could not oppose their powerful foes,
    The conquering British troops, sir.

From morn to night these men of might
    Displayed amazing courage;
And when the sun was fairly down,
    Retired to sup their porrage.

An hundred men with each a pen,
    Or more, upon my word, sir.
It is most true would be too few,
    Their valor to record, sir.

Such feats did they perform that day,
    Against these wicked kegs, sir,
That years to come, if they get home,
    They'll make their boasts and brags, sir.

JONATHAN ODELL [1737-1818]

Odell was the most virulent and powerful if not most skilled of the loyalist satirists, and is most often characterized as the Tory counterpart to Philip Freneau.

Although descendant of one of the founders of the Massachusetts colony, Odell was violently opposed to any extra-legal assertion of American rights against the British crown. His strong pro-English views, as typified by his "A Birthday Song" in honor of King George in 1777, at the very time of soaring national passions, required him to seek and obtain protection from the British army.

After the defeat of Cornwallis is 1781, he spurned reconciliation and encouraged continued hostilities. After the peace, he fled to Nova Scotia rather than accept American independence. He became so repugnant and odious to his contemporaries that even his verse was omitted from anthologies of the time and well into the next century.

A Birthday Song [*1777*]

For the King's Birthday, June 4, 1777

Time was when America hallowed the morn
On which the loved monarch of Britain was born,
Hallowed the day, and joyfully chanted
    God save the King!

Then flourished the blessings of freedom and peace,
And plenty flowed in with a yearly increase.
Proud of our lot we chanted merrily
    Glory and joy crown the King!

With envy beheld by the nations around,
We rapidly grew, nor was anything found
Able to check our growth while we chanted
    God save the King!
O blest beyond measure, had honor and truth
Still nursed in our hearts what they planted in youth!
Loyalty still had chanted merrily
    Glory and joy crown the King!

But see! how rebellion has lifted her head!
How honor and truth are with loyalty fled!
Few are there now who join us in chanting
    God save the King!
And see! how deluded the multitude fly
To arm in a cause that is built on a lie!
Yet are we proud to chant thus merrily
    Glory and joy crown the King!

Though faction by falsehood awhile may prevail,
And loyalty suffers a captive in jail,
Britain is roused, rebellion is falling:
    God save the King!
The captive shall soon be released from his chain;
And conquest restore us to Britain again,
Ever to join in chanting merrily
    Glory and joy crown the King!

The American Times, selections [*1780*]

Hear thy indictment, Washington, at large;
Attend and listen to the solemn charge:
Thou hast supported an atrocious cause
Against thy King, thy Country, and the laws;
Committed perjury, encourag'd lies,
Forced conscience, broken the most sacred ties;
Myriads of wives and fathers at thy hand
Their slaughter'd husbands, slaughter'd sons demand;
That pastures hear no more the lowing kine,
That towns are desolate, all, all is thine;
The frequent sacrilege that pain'd my sight,
The blasphemies my pen abhors to write,
Innumerable crimes on thee must fall,
For thou maintainest, thou defendest all.
    Wilt thou pretend that Britain is in fault?
In Reason's court a falsehood goes for nought.
Will it avail, with subterfuge refin'd,
To say such deeds are foreign to thy mind?
Wilt thou assert that, generous and humane,
Thy nature suffers at another's pain?
He who a band of ruffians keeps to kill,
Is he not guilty of the blood they spill?
Who guards M'Kean and Joseph Reed the vile,

Help'd he not murder Roberts and Carlisle?
So, who protects committees in the chair,
In all their shocking cruelties must share.
   What could, when half-way up the hill to fame,
Induce thee to go back and link with shame?
Was it ambition, vanity, or spite,
That prompted thee with Congress to unite?
Or did all three within they bosom roll,
"Thou heart of hero with a traitor's soul"?
Go, wretched author of thy country's grief,
Patron of villainy, of villains chief;
Seek with thy cursed crew the central gloom,
Ere Truth's avenging sword begin thy doom,
Or sudden vengeance of celestial dart
Precipitate thee with augmented smart!

HUGH HENRY BRACKENRIDGE [1748-1816]

Author of one of the most important dramatic poems of the Revolution, Brackenridge was a tutor, preacher, editor, lawyer, Revolutionary army chaplin, and judge.

"The Battle of Bunker Hill" was written to inspire the rebels with confidence by portraying their remarkable military prowess, and underscoring the moral superiority of their cause.

Brackenridge had also, while a senior at Princeton, collaborated with Philip Freneau on "The Rising Glory of America," a commencement poem celebrating American nationalism and progress.

The Battle of Bunkers-Hill, selections [*1776*]

Act V. Scene I

Bunkers-Hill. Warren with the American Army.

Warren. To arms, brave countrymen! for see, the foe
Comes forth to battle, and would seem to try
Once more their fortune in decisive war.
Three thousand 'gainst seven hundred rang'd this day
Shall give the world an ample specimen
What strength and noble confidence the sound
Of Liberty inspires; that Liberty
Which not the thunder of Bellona's voice,
With fleets and armies from the British Shore,
Shall wrest from us. Our noble ancestors
Out-brav'd the tempests of the hoary deep,
And on these hills uncultivate and wild
Sought an asylum from despotic sway;
A short asylum, for that envious power
With persecution dire still follows us.
At first they deem'd our charters forfeited;
Next our just rights in government abridg'd;
Then thrust in viceroys and bashaws to rule
With lawless sovereignty; now added force
Of standing armies to secure their sway.
Much have we suffer'd from the licens'd rage
Of brutal soldiery in each fair town.
Remember March, brave countrymen, that day
When Boston's streets ran blood! think on that day,
And let the memory to revenge stir up
The temper of your souls! There might we still
On terms precarious and disdainful liv'd,
With daughters ravished and butcher'd sons,
But heaven forbade the thought. These are the men
Who in firm phalanx threaten us with war,
And aim this day to fix forever down
The galling chains which tyranny has forg'd for us.

These count our lands and settlements their own,
And in their intercepted letters speak
Of farms and tenements secur'd for friends;
Which if they gain, brave soldiers, let with blood
The purchase be seal'd down! Let every arm
This day be active in fair freedom's cause,
And shower down from the hill, like Heav'n in wrath,
Full store of light'ning and fierce iron hail
To blast the adversary. Let this ground,
Like burning AEtna or Vesuvius top,
Be wrapt in flame. The word is Liberty;
And Heaven smile on us in so just a cause!

Scene II

Bunkers-Hill. Gardiner, Leading up his Men to the Engagement.
Fear not, brave soldiers, tho' their infantry
In deep array so far out-numbers us:
The justness of our cause will brace each arm
And steel the soul with fortitude, while they,
Whose guilt hangs trembling on their consciences,
Must fail in battle and receive that death
Which in high vengeance we prepare for them.
Let, then, each spirit, to the height wound up,
Shew noble vigour and full force this day,
For on the merit of our swords is plac'd
The virgin honour and true character
Of this whole Continent, and one short hour
May give complexion to the whole event,
Fixing the judgment whether as base slaves
We serve these masters, or more nobly live
Free as the breeze that on the hill-top plays,
With these sweet fields and tenements our own.
Oh fellow soldiers, let this battle speak
Dire disappointment to the insulting foe,
Who claim our fair possessions and set down
These cultur'd farms and bowry hills and plains

As the rich prize of certain victory.
Shall we, the sons of Massachusetts-Bay,
New Hampshire, and Connecticut, shall we
Fall back, dishonour'd, from our native plains,
Mix with the savages and roam for food
On western mountains or the desert shores
Of Canada's cold lakes? or, state more vile,
Sit down in humble vassalage, content
To till the ground for these proud conquerors?
No, fellow soldiers, let us rise this day
Emancipate from such ignoble choice.
And should the battle ravish our sweet lives,
Late time shall give an ample monument
And bid her worthies emulate our fame.

LEMUEL HOPKINS [1750-1801]

Lemuel Hopkins was a leading physician, a founder of the Medical Society of Connecticut, and an established man of letters. A member of the Connecticut Wits, he wrote "The Anarchiad" with John Trumbull and Joel Barlow in which the loose political confederacy of the states prior to the federal constitution is satirized. He wrote or co-authored many satirical poems during his life.

On A Patient Killed By A Cancer Quack

Here lies a fool flat on his back,
The victim of a cancer quack;
Who lost his money and his life,
By plaister, caustic, and by knife.
The case was this—a pimple rose,
South-east a little of his nose;
Which daily redden'd and grew bigger,
As too much drinking gave it vigor;
A score of gossips soon ensure
Full threescore different modes of cure;
But yet the full-fed pimple still
Defied all peticoated skill;
When fortune led him to peruse
A hand-bill in the weekly news;
Sign'd by six fools of different sorts,
All cured of cancers made of warts;
Who recommend, with due submission,
This cancer-monger as magician;
Fear wing'd his flight to find the quack,
And prove his cancer-curing knack;
But on his way he found another,—
A second advertising brother:
But as much like him as an owl
Is unlike every handsome fowl;
Whose fame had raised as broad a fog,
And of the two the greater hog:
Who used a still more magic plaister,
That sweat forsooth, and cured the faster.
This doctor view'd, with moony eyes
And scowl'd-up face, the pimple's size;
Then christen'd it in solemn answer,
And cried, "this pimple's name is cancer.
But courage, friend, I see you're pale,
My sweating plaisters never fail;
I've sweated hundreds out with ease,

With roots as long as maple trees;
And never fail'd in all my trials—
Behold these samples here in vials!
Preserved to show my wondrous merits,
Just as my liver is—in spirits.
For twenty joes the cure is done—"
The bargain struck, the plaister on,
Which gnaw'd the cancer at its leisure,
And pain'd his face above all measure.
But still the pimple spread the faster,
And swell'd, like toad that meets disaster.
Thus foil'd, the doctor gravely swore,
It was a right-rose cancer sore;
Then stuck his probe beneath the beard,
And show'd him where the leaves appear'd;
And raised the patient's drooping spirits,
By praising up the plaister's merits.—
Quoth he, "The roots now scarcely stick—
I'll fetch her out like crab or tick;
And make it rendezvous, next trial,
With six more plagues, in my old vial."
Then purged him pale with jalap drastic,
And next applied the infernal caustic.
But yet, this semblance bright of hell
Served but to make the patient yell;
And, gnawing on with fiery pace,
Devour'd one broadside of his face—
"Courage, 'tis done," the doctor cried,
And quick the incision knife applied:
That with three cuts made such a hole,
Out flew the patient's tortured soul!
    Go, readers, gentle, eke and simple,
If you have wart, or corn, or pimple;
To quack infallible apply;
Here's room enough for you to lie.
His skill triumphant still prevails,
For death's a cure that never fails.

JOHN TRUMBULL [1750-1831]

The brilliant son of a distinguished Connecticut family, Trumbull was a leader of the Connecticut Wits and an established man of letters early in his life, although his literary career was a relatively short one. His controversial "The Progress of Dulness" was written during his tenor as tutor at Yale. The poem is a witty and acrebic criticism of the goals and curriculum of a college education, and the ignorance of the clergy.

Subsequently, however, his literary ambitions were substantially diverted by increasing involvement in the legal profession, and were essentially ended by 1782, when his most successful work, "McFingal," was published.

"McFingal" is a long burlesque epic which lampoons the British and Tories.

The Progress of Dulness [*1772*]

Part I: or the Adventures of Tom Brainless
"Our Tom has grown a sturdy boy;
His progress fills my heart with joy;
A steady soul, that yields no rule,
And quite ingenious too, at school.
Our master says, (I'm sure he's right,)
There's not a lad in town so bright.
He'll cypher bravely, write and read,
And say his catechism and creed,
And scorns to hesitate or falter
In Primer, Spelling-book or Psalter.
Hard work indeed, he does not love it;
His genius is too much above it.
Give him a good substantial teacher,
I'll lay he'd make a special preacher.
I've loved good learning all my life;
We'll send the lad to college, wife,"
          Thus sway'd by fond and sightless passion.
His parents hold a consultation;
If on their couch, or round their fire,
I need not tell, nor you enquire.
     The point's agreed: the boy well pleased,
From country cares and labor eased;
No more to rise by break of day
To drive home cows, or deal out hay;
To work no more in snow or hail,
And blow his fingers o'er the flail,
Or mid the toils of harvest sweat
Beneath the summer's sultry heat,
Serene, he bids the farm, good-bye,
And quits the plough without a sigh.
Propitious to their constant friend,
The pow'rs of idleness attend.

Kind head-ache hail! thou blest disease,
The friend of idleness and ease;
Who mid the still and dreary bound
Where college walls her sons surround,
In spite of fears, in justice' spite,
Assumest o'er laws dispensing right,
Sett'st from his task the blunderer free,
Excused by dulness and by thee.
Thy vot'ries bid a bold defiance
To all the calls and threats of science,
Slight learning human and divine,
And hear no prayers, and fear no fine.
And yet how oft the studious gain,
The dulness of a letter'd brain;
Despising such low things the while,
As English grammar, phrase and style;
Despising ev'ry nicer art,
That aids the tongue, or mends the heart;
Read ancient authors o'er in vain,
Nor taste one beauty they contain;
Humbly on trust accept the sense,
But deal for words at vast expense;
Search well how every term must vary
From Lexicon to Dictionary;
And plodding on in one dull tone,
Gain ancient tongues and lose their own,
Bid every graceful charm defiance,
And woo the skeleton of science.
Come ye, who finer arts despise,
And scoff at verse as heathen lies;
In all the pride of dulness rage
At Pope, or Milton's deathless page;
Or stung by truth's deep-searching line,
Rave ev'n at rhymes as low as mine;
Say ye, who boast the name of wise,
Wherein substantial learning lies.
It is, superb in classic lore,
To speak what Homer spoke before,

To write the language Tully wrote,
The style, the cadence and the note?
Is there a charm in sounds of Greek,
No language else can learn to speak;
That cures distemper'd brains at once,
Like Pliny's rhymes for broken bones?
Is there a spirit found in Latin,
That must evap'rate in translating?
And say are sense and genius bound
To any vehicles of sound?
Can knowledge never reach the brains,
Unless convey'd in ancient strains?
While Homer sets before your eyes
Achilles' rage, Ulysses' lies,
Th' amours of Jove in masquerade,
And Mars entrapp'd by Phoebus' aid;
While Virgil sings, in verses grave,
His lovers meeting in a cave,
His ships turn'd nymphs, in pagan fables,
And how the Trojans eat their tables;
While half this learning but displays
The follies of the former days;
And for our linguists, fairly try them,
A tutor'd parrot might defy them.

Oh! might I live to see that day,
When sense shall point to youths their way;
Through every maze of science guide;
O'er education's laws preside;
The good retain, with just discerning
Explode the quackeries of learning;
Give ancient arts their real due,
Explain their faults, and beauties too;
Teach where to imitate, and mend,
And point their uses and their end.
Then bright philosophy would shine,
And ethics teach the laws divine;
Our youths might learn each nobler art;

That shews a passage to the heart;
From ancient languages well known
Transfuse new beauties to our own;
With taste and fancy well refin'd,
Where moral rapture warms the mind,
From schools dismisse'd, with lib'ral hand,
Spread useful learning o'er the land;
And bid the eastern world admire
Our rising worth, and bright'ning fire.
   But while through fancy's realms we roam,
The main concern is left at home;
Return'd, our hero still we find
The same, as blundering and as blind.
   Four years at college dozed away
In sleep, and slothfulness and play,
Too dull for vice, with clearest conscience,
Charged with no fault but that of nonsense,
And nonsense long, with serious air,
Has wander'd unmolested there,
He passes trial, fair and free,
And takes in form his first degree.
   A scholar see him now commence
Without the aid of books or sense;
For passing college cures the brain,
Like mills to grind men young again.
The scholar-dress, that once array'd him,
The charm, *Admitto te' ad gradum,*
With touch of parchment can refine,
And make the veriest coxcomb shine,
Confer the gift of tongues at once,
And fill with sense the vacant dunce.
So kingly crowns contain quintessence
Of worship, dignity and presence;
Give learning, genius, virtue, worth,
Wit, valor, wisdom, and so forth;
Hide the bald pate, and cover o'er
The cap of folly worn before.

Our hero's wit and learning now may
Be proved by token of diploma,
Of that diploma, which with speed
He learns to construe and to read;
And stalks abroad with conscious stride;
In all the airs of pedant pride,
With passport sign'd for wit and knowledge,
And current under seal of college.
Few months now past, he sees with pain
His purse as empty as his brain;
His father leaves him then to fate,
And throws him off, as useless weight;
But gives him good advice, to teach
A school at first and then to preach.
Thou reason'st well; it must be so;
For nothing else thy son can do.
As thieves of old, t' avoid the halter,
Took refuge in the holy altar;
Oft dulness flying from disgrace
Finds safety in that sacred place;
There boldly rears his head, or rests
Secure from ridicule or jests;
Where dreaded satire may not dare
Offend his wigs' extremest hair;
Where scripture sanctifies his strains,
And reverence hides the want of brains.
Next see our youth at school appear,
Procured for forty pounds a year;
His ragged regiment round assemble,
Taught, not to read, but fear and tremble.
Before him, rods prepare his way,
Those dreaded antidotes to play.
Then throned aloft in elbow chair,
With solemn face and awful air,
He tries, with ease and unconcern,
To teach what ne'er himself could learn;
Gives law and punishment alone,
Judge, jury, bailiff, all in one;
Holds all good learning must depend

Upon his rod's extremest end,
Whose great electric virtue's such,
Each genius brightens at the touch;
With threats and blows, incitements pressing,
Drives on his lads to learn each lesson;
Thinks flogging cures all moral ills,
And breaks their heads to break their wills.
    The year is done; he takes his leave;
The children smile; the parents grieve;
And seek again, their school to keep,
One just as good and just as cheap.
    Now to some priest, that's famed for teaching,
He goes to learn the art of preaching;
And settles down with earnest zeal
Sermons to study, and to steal.
Six months from all the world retires
To kindle up his cover'd fires;
Learns, with nice art, to make with ease
The scriptures speak whate'er he please;
With judgment, unperceived to quote
What Pool explain'd, or Henry wrote;
To give the gospel new editions,
Split doctrines into propositions,
Draw motives, uses, inferences,
And torture words in thousand senses;
Learn the grave style and goodly phrase,
Safe handed down from Cromwell's days,
And shun, with anxious care, the while,
The infection of a modern style;
Or on the wings of folly fly
Aloft in metaphysic sky;
The system of the world explain,
Till night and chaos come again;
Deride what old divines can say,
Point out to heaven a nearer way;
Explode all known establish'd rules,
Affirm our fathers all were fools;
The present age is growing wise,

But wisdom in her cradle lies;
Late, like Minerva, born and bred,
Not from a Jove's, but scribbler's head,
While thousand youths their homage lend her,
And nursing fathers rock and tend her.
Round him much manuscript is spread,
Extracts from living works, and dead,
Themes, sermons, plans of controversy,
That hack and mangle without mercy,
And whence to glad the reader's eyes,
The future dialogue shall rise.
At length, matured the grand design,
He stalks abroad, a grave divine.
Mean while, from every distant seat,
At stated time the clergy meet.
Our hero comes, his sermon reads,
Explains the doctrine of his creeds,
A licence gains to preach and pray,
And makes his bow and goes his way.
What though his wits could ne'er dispense
One page of grammar, or of sense;
What though his learning be so slight,
He scarcely knows to spell or write;
What though his skull be cudgel-proof!
He's orthodox, and that's enough.
Perhaps with genius we'd dispense;
But sure we look at least for sense.
Ye fathers of our church attend
The serious counsels of a friend,
Whose utmost wish, in nobler ways,
Your sacred dignity to raise.
Though blunt the style, the truths set down
Ye can't deny—though some may frown.
Yes, there are men, nor these a few,
The foes of virtue and of you;
Who, nurtured in the scorner's school,
Make vice their trade, and sin by rule;
Who deem it courage heav'n to brave,

And wit, to scoff at all that's grave;
Vent stolen jests, with strange grimaces,
From folly's book of common-places;
While mid the simple throng around
Each kindred blockhead greets the sound,
And, like electric fire, at once,
The laugh is caught from dunce to dunce.
The deist's scoffs ye may despise;
Within yourselves your danger lies;
For who would wish, neglecting rule,
To aid the triumphs of a fool?
From heaven at first your order came,
From heaven received its sacred name,
Indulged to man, to point the way,
That leads from darkness up to day.
Your highborn dignity attend,
And view your origin and end.
    While human souls are all your care,
By warnings, counsels, preaching, prayer,
In bands of christian friendship join'd,
Where pure affection warms the mind,
While each performs the pious race,
Nor dulness e'er usurps a place;
No vice shall brave your awful test,
Nor folly dare to broach the jest,
Each waiting eye shall humbly bend,
And reverence on your steps attend.
    But when each point of serious weight
Is torn with wrangling and debate,
When truth, mid rage of dire divisions,
Is left, to fight for definitions,
And fools assume your sacred place,
It threats your order with disgrace;
Bids genius from your seats withdraw,
And seek the pert, loquacious law;
Or deign in physic's paths to rank,
With every quack and mountebank;
Or in the ways of trade content,

Plod ledgers o'er of cent per cent.
While in your seats so sacred, whence
We look for piety and sense,
Pert dulness raves in school-boy style,
Your friends must blush, your foes will smile;
While men, who teach the glorious way,
Where heaven unfolds celestial day,
Assume the task sublime, to bring
The message of th' Eternal King,
Disgrace those honours they receive,
And want that sense, they aim to give.
    Now in the desk, with solemn air,
Our hero makes his audience stare;
Asserts with all dogmatic boldness,
Where impudence is yoked to dulness;
Reads o'er his notes with halting pace,
Mask'd in the stiffness of his face;
With gestures such as might become
Those statues once that spoke at Rome,
Or Livy's ox, that to the state
Declared the oracles of fate;
In awkward tones, nor said, nor sung,
Slow rumbling o'er the falt'ring tongue,
Two hours his drawling speech holds on,
And names it preaching, when he's done.
    With roving tired, he fixes down
For life, in some unsettled town.
People and priest full well agree,
For why—they know no more than he.
Vast tracts of unknown land he gains,
Better than those the moon contains;
There deals in preaching and in prayer,
And starves on sixty pounds a year,
And culls his texts, and tills his farm,
Does little good, and little harm;
On Sunday, in his best array,
Deals forth the dulness of the day,
And while above he spends his breath,

The yawning audience nod beneath.
Thus glib-tongued Merc'ry in his hand
Stretch'd forth the sleep-compelling wand,
Each eye in endless doze to keep—
The God of speaking, and of sleep.

Part II: of the Life and Character of Dick Hairbrain.

'Twas in a town remote, the place
We leave the reader wise to guess,
(For readers wise can guess full well
What authors never meant to tell,)
There dwelt secure a country clown,
The wealthiest farmer of the town.
Though rich by villany and cheats,
He bought respect by frequent treats;
Gain'd offices by constant seeking,
'Squire, captain, deputy and deacon;
Great was his power, his pride as arrant:
One only son his heir apparent.
He thought the stripling's parts were quick,
And vow'd to make a man of Dick;
Bless'd the pert dunce, and praised his looks,
And put him early to his books.
    More oaths than words Dick learn'd to speak
And studied knavery more than Greek;
Three years at school, as usual, spent,
Then all equipp'd to college went,
And pleased in prospect, thus bestow'd
His meditations, as he rode.
    "All hail, unvex'd with care and strife,
The bliss of academic life;
Where kind repose protracts the span,
While childhood ripens into man;
Where no hard parent's dreaded rage
Curbs the gay sports of youthful age;
Where no vile fear the genius awes
With grim severity of laws;

Where annual troops of bucks come down,
The flower of every neighb'ring town;
Where wealth and pride and riot wait,
And each choice spirit finds his mate.
 "Far from those walls, from pleasure's eye,
Let care and grief and labour fly,
The toil to gain the laurel prize,
That dims the anxious student's eyes,
The pedant air of learned looks,
And long fatigue of turning books.
Let poor dull rogues, with weary pains,
To college come to mend their brains,
And drudge four years, with grave concern
How they may wiser grow, and learn.
Is wealth of indolence afraid,
Or does wit need pedantic aid?
The man of wealth the world descries,
Without the help of learning wise;
The magic powers of gold, with ease,
Transform us to what shape we please,
Give knowledge bright and courage brave,
And sense, that nature never gave.
But nought avails the hoarded treasure;
In spending only lies the pleasure.
 "There vice shall lavish all her charms,
And rapture fold us in her arms,
Riot shall court the frolic soul,
And swearing crown the sparkling bowl;
While wit shall sport with vast applause.
And scorn the feeble tie of laws:
Our midnight joys no rule shall bound,
While games and dalliance revel round.
Such pleasures youthful years can know,
And schools there are, that such bestow.

 Thus reas'ning, Dick goes forth to find
A college suited to his mind;
But bred in distant woods, the clown

Brings all his country airs to town;
The odd address with awkward grace,
That bows with all-averted face;
The half-heard compliments, whose note
Is swallow'd in the trembling throat;
The stiffen'd gait, the drawling tone,
By which his native place is known;
The blush, that looks, by vast degrees,
Too much like modesty to please;
The proud displays of awkward dress,
That all the country fop express,
The suit right gay, though much belated,
Whose fashion's superannuated;
The watch, depending far in state,
Whose iron chain might form a grate;
The silver buckle, dread to view,
O'ershad'wing all the clumsy shoe;
The white-gloved hand, that tries to peep
From ruffle, full five inches deep;
With fifty odd affairs beside,
The foppishness of country pride.
        Poor Dick! though first thy airs provoke
Th' obstreperous laugh and scornful joke,
Doom'd all the ridicule to stand,
While each gay dunce shall lend a hand;
Yet let not scorn dismay thy hope
To shine a witling and a fop.
Blest impudence the prize shall gain,
And bid thee sigh no more in vain.
Thy varied dress shall quickly show
At once the spendthrift and the beau.
With pert address and noisy tongue,
That scorns the fear of prating wrong,
'Mongst list'ning coxcombs shalt thou shine,
And every voice shall echo thine.
        How blest the brainless fop, whose praise
Is doom'd to grace these happy days,
When well-bred vice can genius teach,

And fame is placed in folly's reach,
Impertinence all tastes can hit,
And every rascal is a wit.
　　The lowest dunce, without despairing,
May learn the true sublime of swearing;
Learn the nice art of jests obscene,
While ladies wonder what they mean;
The heroism of brazen lungs,
The rhetoric of eternal tongues;
While whim usurps the name of spirit,
And impudence takes place of merit,
And every money'd clown and dunce
Commences gentleman at once.
　　For now, by easy rules of trade,
Mechanic gentlemen are made!
From handicrafts of fashion born;
Those very arts so much their scorn.
To taylors half themselves they owe,
Who make the clothes, that make the beau.
　　Lo! from the seats, where fops to bless,
Learn'd artists fix the forms of dress,
And sit in consultation grave,
On folded skirt, or strait'ned sleeve,
The coxcomb trips with sprightly haste,
In all the flush of modern taste;
Oft turning, if the day be fair,
To view his shadow's graceful air;
Well pleased with eager eye runs o'er
The laced suit glitt'ring gay before;
The ruffle, where from open'd vest
The rubied brooch adorns the breast;
The coat with length'ning waist behind,
Whose short skirts dangle in the wind;
The modish hat, whose breadth contains
The measure of its owner's brains;
The stockings gay with various hues;
The little toe-encircling shoes;
The cane, on whose carv'd top is shown

An head, just emblem of his own;
While wrapp'd in self, with lofty stride,
His little heart elate with pride,
He struts in all the joys of show,
That taylors give, or beaux can know.
And who for beauty need repine,
That's sold at every barber's sign;
Nor lies in features or complexion,
But curls disposed in meet direction,
With strong pomatum's grateful odour,
And *quantum sufficit* of powder?
These charms can shed a sprightly grace,
O'er the dull eye and clumsy face;
While the trim dancing-master's art
Shall gestures, trips and bows impart,
Give the gay piece its final touches,
And lend those airs, would lure a dutchess.
    Thus shines the form, nor aught behind,
The gifts that deck the coxcomb's mind;
Then hear the daring muse disclose
The sense and piety of beaux.
    To grace his speech, let France bestow
A set of compliments for show.
Land of politeness! that affords
The treasure of new-fangled words,
And endless quantities disburses
Of bows and compliments and curses;
The soft address, with airs so sweet,
That cringes at the ladies' feet;
The pert, vivacious, play-house style,
That wakes the gay assembly's smile;
Jests that his brother beaux may hit,
And pass with young coquettes for wit,
And prized by fops of true discerning,
Outface the pedantry of learning.
Yet learning too shall lend its aid,
To fill the coxcomb's spongy head,
And studious oft he shall peruse

The labours of the modern muse.
From endless loads of novels gain
Soft, simp'ring tales of amorous pain,
With double meanings, neat and handy,
From Rochester and Tristram Shandy.
The blund'ring aid of weak reviews,
That forge the fetters of the muse,
Shall give him airs of criticising
On faults of books, he ne'er set eyes on.
The magazines shall teach the fashion,
And common-place of conversation,
And where his knowledge fails, afford
The aid of many a sounding word.
     Then least religion he should need,
Of pious Hume he'll learn his creed,
By strongest demonstration shown,
Evince that nothing can be known;
Take arguments, unvex'd by doubt,
On Voltaire's trust, or go without;
'Gainst scripture rail in modern lore,
As thousand fools have rail'd before;
Or pleased a nicer art display
T' expound its doctrines all away,
Suit it to modern tastes and fashions
By various notes and emendations;
The rules the ten commands contain,
With new provisos well explain;
Prove all religion was but fashion,
Beneath the Jewish dispensation.

     Blest be his ashes! under ground
If any particles be found,
Who friendly to the coxcomb race,
First taught those arts of common-place,
Those topics fine, on which the beau
May all his little wits bestow,
Secure the simple laugh to raise,
And gain the dunce's palm of praise.

For where's the theme that beaux could hit
With least similitude of wit,
Did not religion and the priest
Supply materials for the jest?
The poor in purse, with metals vile
For current coins, the world beguile;
The poor in brain, for genuine wit
Pass off a viler counterfeit;
While various thus their doom appears,
These lose their souls, and those their ears;
The want of fancy, whim supplies,
And native humour, mad caprice;
Loud noise for argument goes off,
For mirth polite, the ribald's scoff;
For sense, lewd droll'ries entertain us,
And wit is mimick'd by profaneness.
     Thus 'twixt the taylor and the player,
And Hume, and Tristram, and Voltaire,
Complete the modern trim array'd,
The clockwork gentleman is made;
As thousand fops ere Dick have shone,
In airs, which Dick ere long shall own.
     But not immediate from the clown,
He gains this zenith of renown;
Slow dawns the coxcomb's op'ning ray;
Rome was not finish'd in a day.
Perfection is the work of time;
Gradual he mounts the height sublime;
First shines abroad with bolder grace,
In suits of second-handed lace,
And learns by rote, like studious players,
The fop's infinity of airs;
Till merit, to full ripeness grown,
By constancy attains the crown.
     Now should our tale at large proceed,
Here might I tell, and you might read
At College next how Dick went on,
And prated much and studied none;

Yet shone with fair, unborrow'd ray,
And steer'd where nature led the way.
What though each academic science
Bade all his efforts bold defiance!
What though in algebra his station
Was negative in each equation;
Though in astronomy survey'd,
His constant course was retrograde;
O'er Newton's system though he sleeps
And finds his wits in dark eclipse!
His talents proved of highest price
At all the arts of cards and dice;
His genius turn'd, with greatest skill,
To whist, loo, cribbage and quadrille,
And taught, to every rival's shame,
Each nice distinction of the game.
　　As noon-day sun, the case is plain,
Nature has nothing made in vain.
The blind mole cannot fly; 'tis found
His genius leads him under ground.
The man that was not made to think,
Was born to game, and swear, and drink.
Let fops defiance bid to satire,
Mind Tully's rule, and follow nature.
　　Yet here the muse, of Dick, must tell
He shone in active scenes as well;
The foremost place in riots held,
In all the gifts of noice excell'd,
His tongue, the bell, whose rattling din would
Summon the rake's nocturnal synod;
Swore with a grace that seem'd design'd
To emulate the infernal kind,
Nor only make their realms his due,
But learn, betimes, their language too;
And well expert in arts polite,
Drank wine by quarts to mend his sight,
For he that drinks till all things reel,
Sees double, and that's twice as well;

And ere its force confined his feet,
Led out his mob to scour the street;
Made all authority his may-game,
And strain'd his little wits to plague 'em.
Then, every crime atoned with ease,
Pro meritis, received degrees;
And soon, as fortune chanced to fall,
His father died and left him all.
Then bent to gain all modern fashions,
He sail'd to visit foreign nations,
Resolved, but toil unaw'd, to import
The follies of the British court;
But in his course o'erlook'd whate'er
Was learn'd or valued, rich or rare.
    As fire electric draws together
Each hair and straw and dust and feather,
The travell'd dunce collects betimes
The levities of other climes;
And when long toil has given success,
Returns his native land to bless,
A patriot fop, that struts by rules,
And Knight of all the shire of fools.
    The praise of other learning lost,
To know the world is all his boast,
By conduct teach our country widgeons,
How coxcombs shine in other regions,
Display his travell'd airs and fashions,
And scoff at college educations.
    Whoe'er at college points his sneer,
Proves that himself learn'd nothing there,
And wisely makes his honest aim
To pay the mutual debt of shame.
    Mean while our hero's anxious care
Was all employ'd to please the fair;
With vows of love and airs polite,
Oft sighing at some lady's feet;
Pleased, while he thus in form address'd her,
With his own gracefulness of gesture,

And gaudy flattery, that displays
A studied elegance of phrase.
So gay at balls the coxcomb shone,
He thought the female world his own.
By beauty's charms he ne'er was fired;
He flatter'd where the world admired.
Himself, so well he prized desert,
Possest his own unrivall'd heart;
Nor charms, nor chance, nor change could move
The firm foundations of his love;
His heart, so constant and so wise,
Pursued what sages old advise,
Bad others seek for fame or pelf;
His only study was himself.
    Yet Dick allow'd the fair, desert,
Nor wholly scorn'd them in his heart;
There was an end, as oft he said,
For which alone the sex were made,
Whereto, of nature's rules observant,
He strove to render them subservient;
And held the fair by inclination,
Were form'd exactly for their station,
That real virtue ne'er could find
Her lodging in a female mind;
Quoted from Pope, in phrase so smart,
That all the sex are 'rakes at heart,'
And praised Mahomet's sense, who holds
That women ne'er were born with souls.
    Thus blest, our hero saw his name
Rank'd in the foremost lists of fame.
What though the learn'd, the good, the wise,
His light affected airs despise!
What though the fair of higher mind,
With brighter thought and sense refined,
Whose fancy rose on nobler wing,
Scorn'd the vain, gilt, gay, noisy thing!
Each light coquette spread forth her charms,
And lured the hero to her arms.
For beaux and light coquettes, by fate

Were each design'd the other's mate,
By instinct love, for each may find
Its likeness in the other's mind.
    Each gayer fop of modern days
Allow'd to Dick the foremost praise,
Borrow'd his style, his airs, grimace,
And aped his modish form of dress.
Even some, with sense endued, felt hopes
And warm ambition to be fops:
But men of sense, 'tis fix'd by fate,
Are coxcombs but of second rate.
The pert and lively dunce alone
Can steer the course that Dick has shown;
The lively dunce alone can climb
The summit, where he shines sublime.
    But ah! how short the fairest name
Stands on the slippery steep of fame!
The noblest heights we're soonest giddy on;
The sun ne'er stays in his meridian;
The brightest stars must quickly set;
And Dick has deeply run in debt.
Not all his oaths can duns dismay,
Or deadly bailiffs fright away,
Not all his compliments can bail,
Or minuets dance him from the jail.
Law not the least respect can give
To the laced coat, or ruffled sleeve;
His splendid ornaments must fall,
And all is lost, for these were all.
    What then remains? in health's decline,
By lewdness, luxury and wine,
Worn by disease, with purse too shallow,
To lead in fashions, or to follow,
The meteor's gaudy light is gone;
Lone age with hasty step comes on.
How pale the palsied fop appears,
Low shivering in the vale of years;
The ghost of all his former days,

When folly lent the ear of praise,
And beaux with pleased attention hung
On accents of his chatt'ring tongue.
Now all those days of pleasure o'er,
That chatt'ring tongue must prate no more.
From every place, that bless'd his hopes,
He's elbow'd out by younger fops.
Each pleasing thought unknown, that cheers
The sadness of declining years,
In lonely age he sinks forlorn,
Of all, and even himself, the scorn.
    The coxcomb's course were gay and clever,
Would health and money last for ever,
Did conscience never break the charm,
Nor fear the future worlds alarm.
But oh, since youth and years decay,
And life's vain follies fleet away,
Since age has no respect for beaux,
And death the gaudy scene must close,
Happy the man, whose early bloom
Provides for endless years to come;
That learning seeks, whose useful gain
Repays the course of studious pain,
Whose fame the thankful age shall raise,
And future times repeat its praise;
Attains that heart-felt peace of mind,
To all the will of heaven resign'd,
Which calms in youth, the blast of rage,
Adds sweetest hope to sinking age,
With valued use prolongs the breath,
And gives a placid smile to death.

Part III: or the Adventures of Miss Harriet Simper.

"Come hither, Harriet, pretty Miss;
Come hither; give your aunt a kiss.
What, blushing? fye, hold up your head,
Full six years old and yet afraid!

With such a form, an air, a grace,
You're not ashamed to show your face!
Look like a lady—bold—my child!
Why ma'am, your Harriet will be spoil'd.
What pity 'tis, a girl so sprightly
Should hang her head so unpolitely?
And sure there's nothing worth a rush in
That odd, unnatural trick of blushing;
It marks one ungenteelly bred,
And shows there's mischief in her head.
I've heard Dick Hairbrain prove from Paul,
Eve never blush'd before the fall.
'Tis said indeed, in latter days,
It gain'd our grandmothers some praise;
Perhaps it suited well enough
With hoop and farthingale and ruff;
But this politer generation
Holds ruffs and blushes out of fashion.

   "And what can mean your simple whim here
To keep her poring on his primer?
'Tis quite enough for girls to know,
If she can read a billet-doux,
Or write a line you'd understand
Without a cypher of the hand.
Why need she learn to write, or spell?
A pothook scrawl is just as well;
Might rank her with the better sort,
For 'tis the reigning mode at court.
And why should girls be learn'd or wise?
Books only serve to spoil their eyes.
The studious eye but faintly twinkles,
And reading paves the way to wrinkles.
In vain may learning fill the head full;
'Tis beauty that's the one thing needful;
Beauty, our sex's sole pretence,
The best receipt for female sense,
The charm that turns all words to witty,

And makes the silliest speeches pretty.
Ev'n folly borrows killing graces
From ruby lips and roseate faces.
Give airs and beauty to your daughter,
And sense and wit will follow after."
    Thus round the infant Miss in state
The council of the ladies meet,
And gay in modern style and fashion
Prescribe their rules of education.
The mother once herself a toast,
Prays for her child the self-same post;
The father hates the toil and pother,
And leaves his daughters to their mother;
From whom her faults, that never vary,
May come by right hereditary,
Follies be multiplied with quickness,
And whims keep us the family likeness.

    Thus Harriet, rising on the stage,
Learns all the arts, that please the age,
And studies well, as fits her station,
The trade and politics of fashion:
A judge of modes in silks and satins,
From tassels down to clogs and pattens;
A genius, that can calculate
When modes of dress are out of date,
Cast the nativity with ease
Of gowns, and sacks and negligees,
And tell, exact to half of a minute,
What's out of fashion and what's in it;
And scanning all with curious eye,
Minutest faults in dresses spy;
(So in nice points of sight, a flea
Sees atoms better far than we;)
A patriot too, she greatly labours,
To spread her arts among her neighbours,
Holds correspondences to learn
What facts the female world concern,

To gain authentic state-reports
Of varied modes in distant courts,
The present state and swift decays
Of tuckers, handkerchiefs and stays,
The colour'd silk that beauty wraps,
And all the rise and fall of caps.
Then shines, a pattern to the fair,
Of mien, address and modish air,
Of every new, affected grace,
That plays the eye, or decks the face,
The artful smile, that beauty warms,
And all th' hypocrisy of charms.
On Sunday, see the haughty maid
In all the glare of dress array'd,
Deck'd in her most fantastic gown,
Because a stranger's come to town.
Heedless at church she spends the day,
For homelier folks may serve to pray,
And for devotion those may go,
Who can have nothing else to do.
Beauties at church must spend their care in
Far other work, than pious hearing;
They've beaux to conquer, belles to rival;
To make them serious were uncivil.
For, like the preacher, they each Sunday
Must do their whole week's work in one day.

Yet that we fairly may proceed,
We own that ladies sometimes read,
And grieve, that reading is confin'd
To books that poison all the mind;
Novels and plays, (where shines display'd
A world that nature never made,)
Which swell their hopes with airy fancies,
And amorous follies of romances;
Inspire with dreams the witless maiden
On flowery vales and fields Arcadian,
And constant hearts no chance can sever,

And mortal loves, that last for ever.
  For while she reads romance, the fair one
Fails not to think herself the heroine;
For every glance, or smile, or grace,
She finds resemblance in her face,
Expects the world to fall before her,
And every fop she meets adore her.
Thus Harriet reads, and reading really
Believes herself a young Pamela,
The high-wrought whim, the tender strain
Elate her mind and turn her brain:
Before her glass, with smiling grace,
She views the wonders of her face;
There stands in admiration moveless,
And hopes a Grandison, or Lovelace.
  Then shines she forth, and round her hovers
The powder'd swarm of bowing lovers;
By flames of love attracted thither,
Fops, scholars, dunces, cits, together.
No lamp exposed in nightly skies,
E'er gather'd such a swarm of flies;
Or flame in tube electric draws
Such thronging multitudes of straws.
(For I shall still take similes
From fire electric when I please.)
  With vast confusion swells the sound,
When all the coxcombs flutter round.
What undulation wide of bows!
What gentle oaths and am'rous vows!
What double entendres all so smart!
What sighs hot-piping from the heart!
What jealous leers! what angry brawls
To gain the lady's hand at balls!
What billet-doux, brimful of flame!
Acrostics lined with Harriet's name!
What compliments, o'er-strain'd with telling
Sad lies of Venus and of Helen!

What wits half-crack'd with commonplaces
On angels, goddesses and graces!
On fires of love what witty puns!
What similes of stars and suns!
What cringing, dancing, ogling, sighing,
What languishing for love, and dying!

'Twould weary all the pow'rs of verse
Their amorous speeches to rehearse,
Their compliments, whose vain parade
Turns Venus to a kitchen-maid;
With high pretence of love and honor,
They vent their folly all upon her.
(Ev'n as the scripture precept saith,
More shall be given to him that hath;)
Tell her how wond'rous fair they deem her,
How handsome all the world esteem her;
And while they flatter and adore,
She contradicts to call for more.
    "And did they say I was so handsome?
My looks—I'm sure no one can fancy 'em.
'Tis true we're all as we were framed,
And none have right to be ashamed;
But as for beauty—all can tell
I never fancied I look'd well;
I were a fright, had I a grain less.
You're only joking, Mr. Brainless."
    Yet beauty still maintain'd her sway,
And bade the proudest hearts obey;
Ev'n sense her glances could beguile,
And vanquish'd wisdom with a smile;
While merit bow'd and found no arms,
To oppose the conquests of her charms,
Caught all those bashful fears, that place
The mask of folly on the face,
That awe, that robs our airs of ease,
And blunders, when it hopes to please;

For men of sense will always prove
The most forlorn of fools in love.
The fair esteem'd, admired, 'tis true,
And praised—'tis all coquettes can do.
   And when deserving lovers came,
Believed her smiles and own'd their flame,
Her bosom thrill'd, with joy affected
T' increase the list, she had rejected;
While pleased to see her arts prevail,
To each she told the self-same tale.
She wish'd in truth they ne'er had seen her,
And feign'd what grief it oft had giv'n her.
And sad, of tender-hearted make,
Grieved they were ruin'd for her sake.
'Twas true, she own'd on recollection,
She'd shown them proofs of kind affection:
But they mistook her whole intent,
For friendship was the thing she meant.

   But now the time was come, our fair
Should all the plagues of passion share,
And after ev'ry heart she'd won,
By sad disaster lose her own.
So true the ancient proverb sayeth,
'Edge-tools are dang'rous things to play with;
The fisher, ev'ry gudgeon hooking,
May chance himself to catch a ducking;
The child that plays with fire, in pain
Will burn its fingers now and then.
And from the dutchess to the laundress,
Coquettes are seldom salamanders.
      For lo! Dick Hairbrain heaves in sight,
From foreign climes returning bright;
He danced, he sung to admiration,
He swore to gen'ral acceptation,
In airs and dress so great his merit,
He shone—no lady's eyes could bear it.

Poor Harriet saw; her heart was stouter;
She gather'd all her smiles about her;
Hoped by her eyes to gain the laurels,
And charm him down, as snakes do squirrels,
So prized his love and wish'd to win it,
And took such pains his heart to move.
Herself fell desp'rately in love;
Though great her skill in am'rous tricks.
She could not hope to equal Dick's:
Her fate she ventured on his trial.
And lost her birthright of denial.
    And here her brightest hopes miscarry;
For Dick was too gallant to marry.
He own'd she'd charms for those who need 'em,
But he, be sure, was all for freedom;
So, left in hopeless flames to burn,
Gay Dick esteem'd her in her turn.
In love, a lady once given over
Is never fated to recover,
Doom'd to indulge her troubled fancies,
And feed her passion by romances;
And always amorous, always changing,
From coxcomb still to coxcomb ranging,
Finds in her heart a void, which still
Succeeding beaux can never fill:
As shadows vary o'er a glass,
Each holds in turn the vacant place;
She doats upon her earliest pain,
And following thousands loves in vain.
    Poor Harriet now hath had her day;
No more the beaux confess her sway;
New beauties push her from the stage;
She trembles at th' approach of age,
And starts to view the alter'd face,
That wrinkles at her in her glass:
So Satan, in the monk's tradition,
Fear'd, when he met his apparition.

At length her name each coxcomb cancels
From standing lists of toasts and angels;
And slighted where she shone before,
A grace and goddess now no more,
Despised by all, and doom'd to meet
Her lovers at her rival's feet,
She flies assemblies, shuns the ball,
And cries out, vanity, on all;
Affects to scorn the tinsel-shows
Of glittering belles and gaudy beaux;
Nor longer hopes to hide by dress
The tracks of age upon her face.
Now careless grown of airs polite,
Her noonday nightcap meets the sight:
Her hair uncomb'd collects together,
With ornaments of many a feather;
Her stays for easiness thrown by,
Her rumpled handkerchief awry,
A careless figure half undress'd,
(The reader's wits may guess the rest;)
All points of dress and neatness carried,
As though she'd been a twelvemonth married:
She spends her breath, as years prevail,
At this sad wicked world to rail,
To slander all her sex *impromptu*,
And wonder what the times will come to.
        Tom Brainless, at the close of last year,
Had been six years a rev'rend Pastor,
And now resolved, to smooth his life,
To seek the blessing of a wife.
His brethren saw his amorous temper,
And recommended fair Miss Simper,
Who fond, they heard, of sacred truth,
Had left her levities of youth,
Grown fit for ministerial union,
And grave, as Christian's wife in Bunyan.

On this he rigg'd him in his best,
And got his old grey wig new dress'd,
Fix'd on his suit of sable stuffs,
And brush'd the powder from the cuffs,
With black silk stockings, yet in being,
The same he took his first degree in;
Procured a horse of breed from Europe,
And learn'd to mount him by the stirrup,
And set forth fierce to court the maid;
His white-hair'd Deacon went for aid;
And on the right, in solemn mode,
The Reverend Mr. Brainless rode.
Thus grave, the courtly pair advance,
Like knight and squire in famed romance.
The priest then bow'd in sober gesture,
And all in scripture terms address'd her;
He'd found, for reasons amply known,
It was not good to be alone,
And thought his duty led to trying
The great command of multiplying;
So with submission, by her leave,
He'd come to look him out an Eve,
And hoped, in pilgrimage of life,
To find an helpmate in a wife,
A wife discreet and fair withal,
To make amends for Adam's fall.
    In short, the bargain finish'd soon,
A reverend Doctor made them one.
    And now the joyful people rouze all
To celebrate their priest's espousal;
And first, by kind agreement set,
In case their priest a wife could get,
The parish vote him five pounds clear,
T' increase his salary every year.
Then swift the tag-rag gentry come
To welcome Madam Brainless home;
Wish their good Parson joy; with pride
In order round salute the bride;
At home, at visits and at meetings,

To Madam all allow precedence;
Greet her at church with rev'rence due,
And next the pulpit fix her pew.

M'Fingal, selections [*1776, 1781*]

Canto I

The Town-Meeting, A.M.

When Yankees, skilled in martial rule,
First put the British troops to school:
Instructed them in warlike trade,
And new manœuvres of parade,
The true war-dance of Yankee reels,
And *manual exercise* of heels;
Made them give up, like saints complete,
The arm of flesh, and trust the feet,
And work, like Christians undissembling,
Salvation out, by fear and trembling;
Taught Percy fashionable races,
And modern modes of Chevy-Chases:
From Boston, in his best array,
Great 'Squire M'Fingal took his way,
And graced with ensigns of renown,
Steered homeward to his native town.
   His high descent our heralds trace
From Ossian's famed Fingalian race:
For though their name some part may lack,
Old Fingal spelt it with a Mac;
Which great M'Pherson, with submission,
We hope will add the next addition.
   His fathers flourished in the Highlands
Of Scotia's fog-benighted islands;
Whence gained our 'Squire two gifts by right,
Rebellion and the Second-sight.
Of these, the first, in ancient days,
Had gained the noblest palm of praise,

'Gainst kings stood forth and many a crowned head
With terror of its might confounded;
Till rose a king with potent charm
His foes by meekness to disarm,
Whom every Scot and Jacobite
Straight fell in love with at first sight;
Whose gracious speech with aid of pensions,
Hushed down all murmurs of dissensions,
And with the sound of potent metal
Brought all their buzzing swarms to settle;
Who rained his ministerial manna,
Till loud Sedition sund hosanna;
The grave Lords-Bishops and the Kirk
United in the public work;
Rebellion, from the northern regions,
With Bute and Mansfield swore allegiance;
All hands combined to raze, as nuisance,
Of church and state the Constitutions,
Pull down the empire, on whose ruins
They meant to edify their new ones;
Enslave th' American wildernesses,
And rend the provinces in pieces.
With these our 'Squire, among the valiant'st,
Employed his time and tools and talents,
And found this new rebellion pleasing
As his old king-destroying treason.
    Nor less availed his optic sleight,
And Scottish gift of second-sight.
No ancient sybil, famed in rhyme,
Saw deeper in the womb of time;
No block in old Dodona's grove
Could ever more orac'lar prove.
Not only saw he all that could be,
But much that never was, nor would be;
Whereby all prophets far outwent he,
Though former days produced a plenty:
For any man with half an eye
What stands before him can espy;

But optics sharp it needs, I ween,
To see what is not to be seen.
As in the days of ancient fame,
Prophets and poets were the same,
And all the praise that poets gain
Is for the tales they forge and feign;
So gained our 'Squire his fame by seeing
Such things as never would have being;
Whence he for oracles was grown
The very tripod of his town.
Gazettes no sooner rose a lie in,
But straight he fell to prophesying;
Made dreadful slaughter in his course,
O'erthrew provincials, foot and horse,
Brought armies o'er, by sudden pressings,
Of Hanoverians, Swiss, and Hessians,
Feasted with blood his Scottish clan,
And hanged all rebels to a man,
Divided their estates and pelf,
And took a goodly share himself.
All this with spirit energetic,
He did by second-sight prophetic.
   Thus stored with intellectual riches,
Skilled was our 'Squire in making speeches;
Where strength of brains united centers
With strength of lungs surpassing Stentor's.
But as some muskets so contrive it,
As oft to miss the mark they drive at,
And though well aimed at duck or plover,
Bear wide, and kick their owners over:
So fared our 'Squire, whose reasoning toil
Would often on himself recoil,
And so much injured more his side,
The stronger arguments he applied;
As old war-elephants, dismayed,
Trod down the troops they came to aid,
And hurt their own side more in battle,
Than less and ordinary cattle.

Yet at Town-meetings every chief
Pinned faith on great M'Fingal's sleeve;
Which when he lifted, all by rote
Raised sympathetic hands to vote.
   The Town, our hero's scene of action,
Had long been torn by feuds of faction,
And as each party's strength prevails,
It turned up different, heads or tails;
With constant rattling, in a trice,
Showed various sides, as oft as dice.
As that famed weaver, wife t' Ulysses,
By night her day's work picked in pieces,
And though she stoutly did bestir her,
Its finishing was ne'er the nearer:
So did this town with ardent zeal
Weave cobwebs for the public weal,
Which, when completed, or before,
A second vote in pieces tore.
They met, made speeches full long-winded,
Resolved, protested, and rescinded;
Addresses signed; then chose committees
To stop all drinking of Bohea teas;
With winds of doctrine veered about,
And turned all Whig committees out.
Meanwhile our Hero, as their head,
In pomp the Tory faction led,
Still following, as the 'Squire should please,
Successive on, like files of geese.
   And now the town was summoned, greeting,
To grand parading of Town-meeting;
A show, that strangers might appal,
As Rome's grave senate did the Gaul.
High o'er the rout, on pulpit stairs,
Mid den of thieves in house of prayers,
(That house, which loth a rule to break
Served heaven, but one day in the week,
Open the rest for all supplies
Of news, and politics, and lies;)

Stood forth the Constable; and bore
His staff, like Mercury's wand of yore,
Waved potent round, the peace to keep,
As that laid dead men's souls to sleep.
Above and near th' hermetic staff,
The Moderator's upper half
In grandeur o'er the cushion bowed,
Like Sol half seen behind a cloud,
Beneath stood voters of all colors,
Whigs, Tories, orators, and brawlers;
With every tongue in either faction
Prepared like minute-men for action;
Where truth and falsehood, wrong and right,
Drew all their legions forth to fight.
With equal uproar scarcely rave
Opposing winds in AEolus' cave;
Such dialogues with earnest face
Held never Balaam with his ass.

Canto III

The Liberty-Pole

This said, our 'Squire, yet undismayed,
Called forth the Constable to aid,
And bade him read, in nearer station,
The Riot-act and Proclamation.
He swift, advancing to the ring,
Began, "Our Sovereign Lord, the King"—
When thousand clamorous tongues he hears,
And clubs and stones assail his ears.
To fly was vain; to fight was idle;
By foes encompassed in the middle,
His hope, in stratagems, he found,
And fell right craftily to ground;
Then crept to seek an hiding place,
'Twas all he could, beneath a brace;
Where soon the conquering crew espied him,
And where he lurked, they caught and tied him.

At once with resolution fatal,
Both Whigs and Tories rushed to battle.
Instead of weapons, either band
Seized on such arms as came to hand.
And as famed Ovid paints th' adventures
Of wrangling Lapithæ and Centaurs,
Who at their feast, by Bacchus led,
Threw bottles at each other's head;
And these arms failing in their scuffles,
Attacked with andirons, tongs, and shovels:
So clubs and billets, staves and stones
Met fierce, encountering every sconce,
And covered o'er with knobs and pains
Each void receptacle for brains;
Their clamors rend the skies around,
The hills rebellow to the sound;
And many a groan increased the din
From battered nose and broken shin.
    M'Fingal, rising at the word,
Drew forth his old militia-sword;
Thrice cried "King George," as erst in distress,
Knights of romance invoked a mistress;
And brandishing the blade in air,
Struck terror through th' opposing war.
The Whigs, unsafe within the wind
Of such commotion, shrunk behind.
With whirling steel around addressed,
Fierce through their thickest throng pressed,
(Who rolled on either side in arch,
Like Red Sea waves in Israel's march)
And like a meteor rushing through,
Struck on their Pole a vengeful blow.
Around, the Whigs, of clubs and stones
Discharged whole volleys, in platoons,
That o'er in whistling fury fly;
But not a foe dares venture nigh.
And now perhaps with glory crowned
Our 'Squire had felled the pole to ground,

Had not some Power, a Whig at heart,
Descended down and took their part,
(Whether 'twere Pallas, Mars, or Iris,
'Tis scarce worth while to make inquiries)
Who at the nick of time alarming,
Assumed the solemn form of Chairman,
Addressed a Whig, in every scene
The stoutest wrestler on the green,
And pointed where the spade was found,
Late used to set their pole in ground,
And urged, with equal arms and might,
To dare our 'Squire to single fight.
The Whig thus armed, untaught to yield,
Advanced tremendous to the field:
Nor did M'Fingal shun the foe,
But stood to brave the desperate blow;
While all the party gazed, suspended
To see the deadly combat ended;
And Jove in equal balance weighed
The sword against the brandished spade,
He weighed; but lighter than a dream,
The sword flew up, and kicked the beam.
Our 'Squire on tiptoe rising fair
Lifts high a noble stroke in air,
Which hung not, but like dreadful engines,
Descended on his foe in vengeance.
But ah! in danger, with dishonor
The sword perfidious fails its owner;
The sword, which oft had stood its ground,
By huge trainbands encircled round;
And on the bench, with blade right loyal,
Had won the day at many a trial,
Of stones and clubs had braved th' alarms,
Shrunk from these new Vulcanian arms.
The spade so tempered from the sledge,
Nor keen nor solid harmed its edge,
Now met it, from his arm of might,
Descending with steep force to smite;

The blade snapped short—and from his hand,
With rust embrowned the glittering sand.
Swift turned M'Fingal at the view,
And called to aid th' attendant crew,
In vain; the Tories all had run,
When scarce the fight was well begun;
Their setting wigs he saw decreased
Far in th' horizon toward the west.
Amazed he viewed the shameful sight,
And saw no refuge, but in flight:
But age unwieldy checked his pace,
Though fear had winged his flying race;
For not a trifling prize at stake;
No less than great M'Fingal's back.
With legs and arms he worked he course,
Like rider that outgoes his horse,
And labored hard to get away, as
Old Satan struggling on through chaos;
'Till looking back, he spied in rear
The spade-armed chief advanced too near:
Then stopped and seized a stone, that lay
An ancient landmark near the way;
Nor shall we as old bards have done,
Affirm it weighed an hundred ton;
But such a stone, as at a shift
A modern might suffice to lift,
Since men, to credit their enigmas,
Are dwindled down to dwarfs and pigmies,
And giants exiled with their cronies
To Brobdignags and Patagonias.
But while our Hero turned him round,
And tugged to raise it from the ground,
The fatal spade discharged a blow
Tremendous on his rear below:
His bent knee failed, and void of strength
Stretched on the ground his manly length.
Like ancient oak o'erturned, he lay,
Or tower to tempests fallen a prey,

Or mountain sunk with all his pines,
Or flower the plow to dust consigns,
And more things else—but all men know 'em,
If slightly versed in epic poem.
At once the crew, at this dread crisis,
Fall on, and bind him, ere he rises;
And with loud shouts and joyful soul,
Conduct him prisoner to the pole.
When now the mob in lucky hour
Had got their enemies in their power,
They first proceed, by grave command,
To take the Constable in hand.
Then from the pole's sublimest top
The active crew let down the rope,
At once its other end in haste bind,
And make it fast upon his waistband;
Till like the earth, as stretched on tenter,
He hung self-balanced on his centre.
Then upwards, all hands hoisting sail,
They swung him, like a keg of ale,
Till to the pinnacle in height
He vaulted, like balloon or kite.
As Socrates of old at first did
To aid philosophy get hoisted,
And found his thoughts flow strangely clear,
Swung in a basket in mid air:
Our culprit thus, in purer sky,
With like advantage raised his eye,
And looking forth in prospect wide,
His Tory errors clearly spied,
And from his elevated station,
With bawling voice began addressing.
   "Good Gentlemen and friends and kin,
For heaven's sake hear, if not for mine!
I here renounce the Pope, the Turks,
The King, the Devil, and all their works;
And will, set me but once at ease,
Turn Whig or Christian, what you please;

And always mind your rules so justly,
Should I live long as old Methus'lah,
I'll never join in British rage,
Nor help Lord North, nor General Gage;
Nor lift my gun in future fights,
Nor take away your Charter-rights;
Nor overcome your new-raised levies,
Destroy your towns, nor burn your navies;
Nor cut your poles down while I've breath,
Though raised more thick than hatchel-teeth;
But leave King George and all his elves
To do their conquering work themselves."
　　This said, they lowered him down in state,
Spread at all points, like falling cat;
But took a vote first on the question,
That they'd accept this full confession,
And to their fellowship and favor,
Restore him on his good behavior.
　　Not so our 'Squire submits to rule,
But stood, heroic as a mule.
"You'll find it all in vain," quoth he,
"To play your rebel tricks on me.
All punishments, the world can render,
Serve only to provoke th' offender;
The will gains strength from treatment horrid,
As hides grow harder when they're curried.
No man e'er felt the halter draw,
With good opinion of the law;
Or held in method orthodox
His love of justice, in the stocks;
Or failed to lose by sheriff's shears
At once his loyalty and ears.
Have you made Murray look less big,
Or smoked old Williams to a Whig?
Did our mobbed Ol'ver quit his station,
Or heed his vows of resignation?
Has Rivington in dread of stripes,
Ceased lying since you stole his types?

And can you think my faith will alter,
By tarring, whipping, or the halter?
I'll stand the worst; for recompense
I trust King George and Providence.
And when with conquest gained I come,
Arrayed in law and terror home,
Ye'll rue this inauspicious morn,
And curse the day when ye were born,
In Job's high style of imprecations,
With all his plagues, without his patience."
Meanwhile beside the pole, the guard
A Bench of Justice had prepared,
Where sitting round in awful sort
The Grand Committee hold their Court;
While all the crew, in silent awe,
Wait from their lips the lore of law.
Few moments with deliberation
They hold the solemn consultation;
When soon in judgment all agree,
And Clerk proclaims the dread decree;
"That 'Squire M'Fingal having grown
The vilest Tory in the town,
And now in full examination
Convicted by his own confession,
Finding no tokens of repentance,
This court proceeds to render sentence:
That first the Mob a slip-knot single
Tie round the neck of said M'Fingal,
And in due form do tar him next,
And feather, as the law directs;
Then through the town attendant ride him
In cart with Constable beside him,
And having held him up to shame,
Bring to the pole, from whence he came."
    Forthwith the crowd proceed to deck
With haltered noose M'Fingal's neck,
While he in peril of his soul

Stood tied half-hanging to the pole;
Then lifted high the ponderous jar,
Poured o'er his head the smoking tar.
With less profusion once was spread
Oil on the Jewish monarch's head,
That down his beard and vestments ran,
And covered all his outward man.
As when (so Claudian sings) the Gods
And earth-born Giants fell at odds,
And stout Enceladus in malice
Tore mountains up to throw at Pallas;
And while he held them o'er his head,
The river, from their fountains fed,
Poured down his back its copious tide,
And wore its channels in his hide:
So from the high-raised urn the torrents
Spread down his side their various currents;
His flowing wig, as next the brim,
First met and drank the sable stream;
Adown his visage stern and grave
Rolled and adhered the viscid wave;
With arms depending as he stood,
Each cuff capacious holds the flood;
From nose and chin's remotest end,
The tarry icicles descend;
Till all o'erspread, with colors gay,
He glitter'd to the western ray,
Like sleet-bound trees in wintry skies,
Or Lapland idol carved in ice.
And now the feather-bag displayed
Is waved in triumph o'er his head,
And clouds him o'er with feathers missive,
And down, upon the tar, adhesive:
Not Maia's son, with wings for ears,
Such plumage round his visage wears;
Nor Milton's six-winged angel gathers
Such superfluity of feathers.
Now all complete appears our 'Squire,
Like Gorgon or Chimæra dire;

Nor more could boast on Plato's plan
To rank among the race of man,
Or prove his claim to human nature,
As a two-legg'd, unfeathered creature.
   Then on the fatal cart, in state
They raised our grand Duumvirate.
And as at Rome a like committee,
Who found an owl within their city,
With solemn rites and grave processions
At every shrine performed lustrations;
And lest infection might take place
From such grim fowl with feathered face,
All Rome attends him through the street
In triumph to his country seat:
With like devotion all the choir
Paraded round our awful 'Squire;
In front the martial music comes
Of horns and fiddles, fifes and drums,
With jingling sound of carriage bells,
And treble creak of rusted wheels.
Behind, the crowd, in lengthened row
With proud procession, closed the show.
And at fit periods every throat
Combined in universal shout;
And hailed great Liberty in chorus,
Or bawled "Confusion to the Tories."
Not louder storm the welkin braves
From clamors of conflicting waves;
Less dire in Lybian wilds the noise
When ravening lions lift their voice;
Or triumphs at town-meetings made,
On passing votes to regulate trade.
   Thus having borne them round the town,
Last at the pole they set them down;
And to the tavern take their way
To end in mirth the festal day.

JOSEPH STANSBURY [1750-1809]

Foremost among the loyalist poets, Stansbury was a skilled and prolific satirist. Like many others of similar persuasion, he disagreed with British colonial policy, but stopped short of carrying resistance to the point of revolution.

Stansbury attempted, before the war, to maintain the American identity with England. After hostilities commenced, he spent most of the war years behind British lines. Although he did write "The Lords of the Main" as a war song for British sailors, it was not aimed at Americans, but rather their allies, the French and Spanish.

Nevertheless, when, after the war, he attempted to re-enter American society by accepting and reconciling himself to the results, he was rebuffed and forced into exile in Nova Scotia.

Eventually he returned to America and spent his last years in relative tranquility.

When Good Queen Elizabeth Governed the Realm [*1774*]

A Song

When good Queen Elizabeth governed the Realm,
And Burleigh's sage counsels directed the helm,
In vain Spain and France our conquests opposed;
For Valor conducted what Wisdom proposed.
    Beef and beer was their food;
    Love and truth armed their band;
    Their courage was ready—
    Steady, boys, steady—
To fight and to conquer by sea and by land.

But since tea and coffee, so much to our grief,
Have taken the place of strong beer and roast beef,
Our laurels have withered, our trophies been torn;
And the lions of England French triumphs adorn.
    Tea and slops are their food;
    They unnerve every hand—
    Their courage unsteady
    And not always ready—
They often are conquered by sea and by land

St. George views with transport our generous flame:
"My sons, rise to glory, and rival my fame.
Ancient manners again in my sons I behold
And this age must eclipse all the ages of gold."
    Beef and beer are our food;
    Love and truth arm our band;
    Our courage is steady
    And always is ready
To fight and to conquer by sea and by land.

While thus we regale as our fathers of old,
Our manners as simple, our courage as bold,
May vigor and prudence our freedom secure
Long as rivers, or ocean, or stars shall endure.
  Beef and beer are our food;
  Love and truth arm our band;
  Our courage is steady
  And always is ready
To fight and to conquer by sea and by land.

The Lords of the Main [*1780*]

When Faction, in league with the treacherous Gaul,
  Began to look big and paraded in state;
A meeting was held at *Credulity Hall,*
  And Echo proclaimed their ally *good and great!*
    By sea and by land
    Such wonders are planned;
No less than the bold British Lion to chain!
    Well hove! says Jack Lanyard,
    French, Congo, and Spaniard,
Have at you—remember we're Lords of the Main!
  Lords of the Main—aye, Lords of the Main;
The tars of Old England are Lords of the Main.

Though party-contention awhile may perplex,
  And lenity hold us in doubtful suspense;
If perfidy rouse, or ingratitude vex,
  In defiance of Hell we'll chastise the offense.
    When danger alarms,
    'Tis then that in arms
United we rush on the foe with disdain:
    And when the storm rages
    It only presages
Fresh triumphs to Britons, as Lords of the Main.
  Lords of the Main—aye, Lords of the Main—
Let *Thunder* proclaim it, we're Lords of the Main.

Then, Britons, *strike home*—make sure of your blow:
   The chase is in view; never mind a lee-shore.
With vengeance o'ertake the confederate foe:
    'Tis now we may rival our heroes of yore!
       Brave Anson and Drake,
       Hawke, Russell, and Blake,
With ardor like your we defy France and Spain!
       Combining with Treason,
       They're deaf to all reason:
Once more let them *feel* we are Lords of the Main.
   Lords of the Main—aye, Lords of the Main—
The first-born of Neptune are Lords of the Main.

Nor are we alone in the noble career;
   The soldier partakes of the generous flame:
To glory he marches, to glory we steer;
    Between us we share the rich harvest of fame.
       Recorded on high,
       Their names never die,
Of heroes by sea and by land what a train!
       To the King, then, God bless him!
       The world shall confess him
"The Lord of those men who are Lords of the Main."
   Lords of the Main—aye, Lords of the Main—
The tars of Old England are Lords of the Main.

Let Us Be Happy As Long As We Can [*1782*]

I've heard in old times that a sage used to say
The seasons were nothing—December or May—
The heat or the cold never entered his plan;
That all should be happy whenever they can.

No matter what power directed the state,
He looked upon such things as ordered by Fate.
Whether governed by many, or ruled by one man,
His rule was—be happy whenever you can.

He happened to enter this world the same day
With the supple, complying, famed Vicar of Bray.
Through both of their lives the same principle ran:
My boys, we'll be happy as long as we can.

Time-serving I hate, yet I see no good reason
A leaf from their book should be thought out of season.
When kicked like a foot-ball from Sheba to Dan,
Egad, let's be happy as long as we can.

Since no one can tell what to-morrow may bring,
Or which side shall triumph, the Congress or King;
Since Fate must o'errule us and carry her plan,
Why, let us be happy as long as we can.

To-night let's enjoy this good wine and a song,
And relish the hour which we cannot prolong.
If evil will come, we'll adhere to our plan,
And baffle misfortune as long as we can.

PHILIP FRENEAU [1752-1832]

America's first major poet, Freneau's literary career, spanning the Revolution and the first third of the Nineteenth Century, was turbulent, vacillant, and dramatic.

A prolific and multi-faceted writer, his poetry ranged from satirical and humorous to romantic and lyrical. He enjoyed periods of great acclaim and popularity, and yet ended his life in relative obscurity (an esteemed poetry anthologist, Samuel Kettell, who had "always been accustomed to hear (him) spoken of as deceased," and published the thought, earned a "splenetic" rebuke from the poet for his negligence).

A mariner, trader, government official, journalist, and patriot, Freneau's patriotic poems, satires of the British, and journalism supporting Jeffersonian democracy represent only a part of the body of work for which he is known. The aspect of literary achievement for which he is remembered in the canon of American letters is that of his lyrical, descriptive, and reflective poetry, what Freneau himself called his "poems of romantic fancy."

The Power of Fancy [*1770*]

Wakeful, vagrant, restless thing,
Ever wandering on the wing,
Who thy wondrous source can find,
Fancy, regent of the mind;
A spark from Jove's resplendent throne,
But thy nature all unknown.

This spark of bright, celestial flame,
From Jove's seraphic altar came,
And hence alone in man we trace,
Resemblance to the immortal race.

Ah! what is all this mighty Whole,
These suns and stars that round us roll!
What are they all, where'er they shine,
But Fancies of the Power Divine!
What is this globe, these lands, and seas,
And heat, and cold, and flowers, and trees,
And life, and death, and beast, and man,
And time,—that with the sun began—
But thoughts on reason's scale combined,
Ideas of the Almighty mind?

On the surface of the brain
Night after night she walks unseen,
Noble fabrics doth she raise
In the woods or on the seas,
On some high, steep, pointed rock,
Where the billows loudly knock
And the dreary tempests sweep
Clouds along the uncivil deep.

Lo! she walks upon the moon,
Listens to the chimy tune
Of the bright, harmonious spheres,
And the song of angels hears;
Sees this earth a distant star,
Pendant, floating in the air;
Leads me to some lonely dome,
Where Religion loves to come,

Where the bride of Jesus dwells,
And the deep toned organ swells
In notes with lofty anthems joined,
Notes that half distract the mind.
  Now like lightning she descends
To the prison of the fiends,
Hears the rattling of their chains,
Feels their never ceasing pains—
But, oh never may she tell
Half the frightfulness of hell.
  Now she views Arcadian rocks,
Where the shepherds guard their flocks,
And, while yet her wings she spreads,
Sees crystal streams and coral beds,
Wanders to some desert deep,
Or some dark, enchanted steep,
By the full moonlight doth shew
Forests of a dusky blue,
Where, upon some mossy bed,
Innocence reclines her head.
  Swift, she stretches o'er the seas
To the far off Hebrides,
Canvas on the lofty mast
Could not travel half so fast—
Swifter than the eagle's flight
Or instantaneous rays of light!
Lo! contemplative she stands
On Norwegia's rocky lands—
Fickle Goddess, set me down
Where the rugged winters frown
Upon Orca's howling steep,
Nodding o'er the northern deep,
Where the winds tumultuous roar,
Vext that Ossian sings no more.
Fancy, to that land repair,
Sweetest Ossian slumbers there;
Waft me far to southern isles
Where the softened winter smiles,

To Bermuda's orange shades,
Or Demarara's lovely glades;
Bear me o'er the sounding cape,
Painting death in every shape,
Where daring Anson spread the sail
Shattered by the stormy gale—
Lo! she leads me wide and far,
Sense can never follow her—
Shape thy course o'er land and sea,
Help me to keep pace with thee,
Lead me to yon chalky cliff,
Over rock and over reef,
Into Britain's fertile land,
Stretching far her proud command.
Look back and view, through many a year,
Cæsar, Julius Cæsar, there.
   Now to Tempe's verdant wood,
Over the mid ocean flood
Lo! the islands of the sea
—Sappho, Lesbos mourns for thee:
Greece, arouse thy humbled head,
Where are all thy might dead,
Who states to endless ruin hurled
And carried vengeance through the world?—
Troy, thy vanished pomp resume,
Or, weeping at thy Hector's tomb,
Yet those faded scenes renew
Whose memory is to Homer due.
Fancy, lead me wandering still
Up to Ida's cloud-topt hill;
Not a laurel there doth grow
But in vision thou shalt show,—
Every sprig on Virgil's tomb
Shall in livelier colors bloom,
And every triumph Rome has seen
Flourish on the years between.
   Now she bears me far away
In the east to meet the day,

Leads me over Ganges' streams,
Mother of the morning beams—
O'er the ocean hath she ran,
Places me on Tinian;
Farther, farther in the east,
Till it almost meets the west,
Let us wandering both be lost
On Taitis sea-beat coast,
Bear me from that distant strand,
Over ocean, over land,
To California's golden shore—
Fancy, stop, and rove no more.
   Now, though late, returning home,
Lead me to Belinda's tomb;
Let me glide as well as you
Through the shroud and coffin too,
And behold, a moment, there,
All that once was good and fair—
Who doth here so soundly sleep?
Shall we break this prison deep?—
Thunders cannot wake the maid,
Lightnings cannot pierce the shade,
And though wintry tempests roar,
Tempests shall disturb no more.
   Yet must those eyes in darkness stay,
That once were rivals to the day—?
Like heaven's bright lamp beneath the main
They are but set to rise again.
   Fancy, thou the muses' pride,
In thy painted realms reside
Endless images of things,
Fluttering each on golden wings,
Ideal objects, such a store,
The universe could hold no more:
Fancy, to thy power I owe
Half my happiness below;
By thee Elysian groves were made,
Thine were the notes that Orpheus played;

By thee was Pluto charmed so well
While rapture seized the sons of hell—
Come, O come—perceived by none,
You and I will walk alone.

A Political Litany [1775]

Librera Nos, Domine.—Deliver us, O Lord, not only from British dependence, but also
From a junto that labor with absolute power,
Whose schemes disappointed have made them look sour,
From the lords of the council, who fight against freedom,
Who still follow on where delusion shall lead them.

From the group at St. James's, who slight our petitions,
And fools that are waiting for further submissions—
From a nation whose manners are rough and severe,
From scoundrels and rascals,—do keep us all clear.

From pirates sent out by command of the king
To murder and plunder, but never to swing.
From Wallace and Greaves, and Vipers and Roses,*
Whom, if heaven pleases, we'll give bloody noses.

From the valiant Dunmore, with his crew of banditti,
Who plunder Virginians at Williamsburg city,
From hot-headed Montague, mighty to swear,
The little fat man with his pretty white hair.

From bishops in Britain, who butchers are grown,
From slaves that would die for a smile from the throne,
From assemblies that vote against Congress proceedings,
(Who now see the fruit of their stupid misleadings.)

From Tryon the mighty, who flies from our city,
And swelled with importance disdains the committee:
(But since his is pleased to proclaim us his foes,
What the devil care we where the devil he goes.)

From the caitiff, lord North, who would bind us in chains,
From a royal king Log, with his tooth-full of brains,
Who dreams, and is certain (when taking a nap)
He has conquered our lands, as they lay on his map.

From a kingdom that bullies, and hectors, and swears,
We send up to heaven our wishes and prayers
That we, disunited, may freemen be still,
And Britain go on—to be damned if she will.

*Captains and ships in the British navy, then employed on the American coast.—
Author's note.

The Vernal Age [*1775*]

Where the pheasant roosts at night,
Lonely, drowsy, out of sight,
Where the evening breezes sigh
Solitary, there stray I.

Close along the shaded stream,
Source of many a youthful dream,
Where branchy cedars dim the day
There I muse, and there I stray.

Yet, what can please amid this bower,
That charmed the eye for many an hour!
The budding leaf is lost to me,
And dead the bloom on every tree.

The winding stream, that glides along,
The lark, that tunes her early song,
The mountain's brow, the sloping vale,
The murmuring of the western gale,

Have lost their charms!—the blooms are gone!
Trees put a darker aspect on,
The stream disgusts that wanders by,
And every zephyr brings a sigh.

Great guardian of our feeble kind!—
Restoring Nature, lend thine aid!
And o'er the features of the mind
Renew those colours, that must fade,
    When vernal suns forbear to roll,
    And endless winter chills the soul.

The House of Night, selections [1775]

By some sad means, when Reason holds no sway,
Lonely I rov'd at midnight o'er a plain
Where murmuring streams and mingling rivers flow
Far to their springs or seek the sea again.

Sweet vernal May! tho' then thy woods in bloom
Flourish'd, yet nought of this could Fancy see;
No wild pinks bless'd the meads, no green the fields,
And naked seem'd to stand each lifeless tree.

Dark was the sky, and not only friendly star
Shone from the zenith or horizon, clear;
Mist sate upon the woods, and darkness rode
In her black chariot with a wild career.

And from the woods the late-resounding note
Issued of the loquacious *Whip-poor-will;*
Hoarse, howling dogs and nightly roving wolves
Clamour'd from far-off clifts invisible.

Rude from the wide-extended *Chesapeke*
I heard the winds the dashing waves assail,
And saw from far, by picturing fancy form'd,
The black ship travelling through the noisy gale.

At last, by chance and guardian fancy led,
I reach'd a noble dome rais'd fair and high,
And saw the light from upper windows flame,
Presage of mirth and hospitality.

And by that light around the dome appear'd
A mournful garden of autumnal hue;
Its lately pleasing flowers all drooping stood
Amidst high weeds that in rank plenty grew.

The Primrose there, the violet darkly blue,
Daisies and fair Narcissus ceas'd to rise;
Gay spotted pinks their charming bloom withdrew,
And Polyanthus quench'd its thousand dyes.

No pleasant fruit or blossom gaily smil'd;
Nought but unhappy plants and trees were seen:
The yew, the myrtle, and the church-yard elm,
The cypress with its melancholy green.

There cedars dark, the osier, and the pine,
Shorn tamarisks, and weeping willows grew,
The poplar tall, the lotos, and the lime;
And pyracantha did her leaves renew.

The poppy there, companion to repose,
Display'd her blossoms that began to fall;
And here the purple amaranthus rose,
With mint strong-scented, for the funeral.

And here and there, with laurel shrubs between,
A tombstone lay, inscrib'd with strains of woe;
And stanzas sad, throughout the dismal green,
Lamented for the dead that slept below.

Peace to this awful dome!—when strait I heard
The voice of men in a secluded room;
Much did they talk of death and much of life,
Of coffins, shrouds, and horrors of a tomb...

Then up three winding stairs my feet were brought
To a high chamber, hung with mourning sad;
The unsnuff'd candles glar'd with visage dim,
'Midst grief in ecstasy of woe run mad.

A wide-leaf'd table stood on either side,
Well fraught with phials, half their liquids spent;
And from a couch behind the curtain's veil
I heard a hollow voice of loud lament.

Turning to view the object whence it came,
My frighted eyes a horrid form survey'd
(*Fancy, I own thy power*): Death on the couch,
With fleshless limbs, at rueful length, was laid.

And o'er his head flew jealousies and cares,
Ghosts, imps, and half the black Tartarian crew,
Arch-angels damn'd; nor was their Prince remote,
Borne on the vaporous wings of Stygian dew.

Around his bed, by the dull flambeaux' glare,
I saw pale phantoms: Rage to madness vext,
Wan, wasting grief, and ever-musing care,
Distressful pain, and poverty perplext.

Sad was his countenance—if we can call
That *countenance* where only bones were seen—
And eyes sunk in their sockets, dark and low,
And teeth that only show'd themselves to grin.

Reft was his scull of hair, and no fresh bloom
Or cheerful mirth sate on his visage hoar:
Sometimes he rais'd his head, while deep-drawn groans
Were mixt with words that did his fate deplore.

Oft did he wish to see the daylight spring;
And often toward the window lean'd to hear,
Fore-runner of the scarlet-mantled morn,
The early note of wakeful *Chanticleer*.....

Then with a hollow voice thus went he on:
"Get up and search, and bring, when found, to me
Some cordial, potion, or some pleasant draught,
Sweet, slumb'rous poppy or the mild Bohea.

"But hark, my pitying friend!—and if you can,
Deceive the grim physician at the door—
Bring half the mountain springs—ah, hither bring
The cold rock-water from the shady bower;

"For till this night such thirst did ne'er invade,
A thirst provok'd by heav'n's avenging hand:
Hence bear me, friends, to quaff and quaff again
The cool wave bubbling from the yellow sand.

"To these dark walls with stately step I came,
Prepar'd your drugs and doses to defy;
Smit with the love of never-dying fame,
I came, alas! to conquer—not to die!"

Glad, from his side I sprang and fetch'd the draught,
Which down his greedy throat he quickly swills;
Then on a second errand sent me strait,
To search in some dark corner for his pills.

Quoth he, "These pills have long compounded been
Of dead men's bones and bitter roots, I trow;
But that I may to wonted health return
Throughout my lank veins shall their substance go."

So down they went.—He rais'd his fainting head,
And oft in feeble tone essay'd to talk:
Quoth he, "Since remedies have small avail,
Assist unhappy Death once more to walk."

Then, slowly rising from his loathsome bed,
On wasted legs the meagre monster stood,
Gap'd wide, and foam'd, and hungry seem'd to ask,
Tho' sick, an endless quantity of food.

Said he, "The sweet melodious flute prepare,
The anthem, and the organ's solemn sound,
Such as may strike my soul with ecstasy,
Such as may from yon' lofty walls rebound.

"Sweet music can the fiercest pains assuage:
She bids the soul to heav'n's blest mansions rise;
She calms despair, controls inernal rage;
And deepest anguish, when it hears her, dies.

"And see, the mizzling, misty midnight reigns,
And no soft dews are on my eye-lids sent:
Here, stranger, lend thy hand, assist me, pray,
To walk a circuit of no large extent."

On my prest shoulders leaning, round he went,
And could have made the boldest spectre flee.
I led him up stairs, and I led him down,
But not one moment's rest from pain got he.....

Up rush'd a band, with compasses and scales
To measure his slim carcase, long and lean.
"Be sure," said he," to frame my coffin strong,
You, master workman, and your men, I mean;

"For if the Devil, so late my trusty friend,
Should get one hint where I am laid, from you,
Not with my soul content, he'd seek to find
That mouldering mass of bones, my body, too!

"Of hardest ebon let the plank be found,
With clamps and ponderous bars secur'd around,
That if the box by Satan should be storm'd
It may be able for resistance found."

"Yes," said the master workman, "noble Death,
Your coffin shall be strong—that leave to me;
But who shall these your funeral dues discharge?
Nor friends nor pence you have, that I can see."

To this said Death, "You might have ask'd me, too,
Base caitiff, who are my executors,
Where my estate, and who the men that shall
Partake my substance and be call'd my heirs.

"Know, then, that hell is my inheritance;
The devil himself my funeral dues must pay:
Go—since you must be paid—go ask of him,
For he has gold, as fabling poets say."

Strait they retir'd—when thus he gave me charge,
Pointing from the light window to the west:
"Go three miles o'er the plain, and you shall see
A burying-yard of sinners dead, unblest.

"Amid the graves a spiry building stands,
Whose solemn knell resounding through the gloom
Shall call thee o'er the circumjacent lands
To the dull mansion destin'd for my tomb.

"There, since 't is dark, I'll plant a glimmering light
Just snatch'd from hell, by whose reflected beams
Thou shalt behold a tomb-stone, full eight feet,
Fast by a grave replete with ghosts and dreams.

"And on that stone engrave this epitaph,
Since Death, it seems, must die like mortal men;
Yes, on that stone engrave this epitaph,
Though all hell's furies aim to snatch the pen:—

"*Death is this tomb his weary bones hath laid,
Sick of dominion o'er the human kind:
Behold what devastations he hath made;
Survey the millions by his arm confin'd.*

"Six thousand years has sovereign sway been mine;
None but myself can real glory claim;
Great Regent of the world I reign'd alone,
And princes trembled when my mandate came.

"Vast and unmatch'd throughout the world, my fame
Takes place of gods, and asks no mortal date—
No, by myself and by the heavens I swear
Not Alexander's name is half so great.

"Nor swords nor darts my prowess could withstand;
All quit their arms and bow'd to my decree:
Even mightly JULIUS *died beneath my hand,*
For slaves and Cæsars were the same to me.

"Traveller, wouldst thou his noblest trophies seek,
Search in no narrow spot obscure for those;
The sea profound, the surface of all land,
Is moulded with the myriads of his foes."....

O'er a dark field I held my dubious way,
Where Jack-a-lanthorn walk'd his lonely round;
Beneath my feet substantial darkness lay,
And screams were heard from the distemper'd ground.

Nor look'd I back, till to a far-off wood,
Trembling with fear, my weary feet had sped:
Dark was the night, but at the inchanted dome
I saw the infernal windows flaming red.

And from within the howls of Death I heard,
Cursing the dismal night that gave him birth,
Damning his ancient sire and mother sin,
Who at the gates of hell, accursed, brought him forth.

(For fancy gave to my enraptur'd soul
An eagle's eye, with keenest glance to see;
And bade those distant sounds distinctly roll,
Which, waking, never had affected me.)

Oft his pale breast with cruel hand he smote,
And, tearing from his limbs a winding-sheet,
Roar'd to the black skies, while the woods around,
As wicked as himself, his words repeat.

Thrice tow'rd the skies his meagre arms he rear'd,
Invok'd all hell and thunders on his head,
Bid light'nings fly, earth yawn, and tempests roar,
And the sea wrap him in its oozy bed.

"My life for one cool draught! O, fetch your springs!
Can one unfeeling to my woes be found?
No friendly visage comes to my relief,
But ghosts impend and spectres hover round.

"Though humbled now, dishearten'd, and distrest,
Yet, when admitted to the peaceful ground,
With heroes, kings, and conquerors I shall rest,
Shall sleep as safely and perhaps as sound."

Dim burnt the lamp; and now the phantom Death
Gave his last groans in horror and despair:
"All hell demands me hence!" he said, and threw
The red lamp hissing through the midnight air.

Trembling, across the plain my course I held,
And found the grave-yard, loitering through the gloom,
And in the midst a hell-red, wandering light,
Walking in fiery circles round the tomb.....

At distance far, approaching to the tomb,
By lamps and lanthorns guided through the shade,
A coal-black chariot hurried through the gloom,
Spectres attending, in black weeds array'd,

Whose woeful forms yet chill my soul with dread:
Each wore a vest in Stygian chambers wove,
Death's kindred all—Death's horses they bestrode,
And gallop'd fiercely, as the chariot drove.

Each horrid face a grizly mask conceal'd;
Their busy eyes shot terror to my soul
As now and then, by the pale lanthorn's glare,
I saw them for their parted friend condole.

Before the horse Death's chaplain seem'd to go,
Who strove to comfort, what he could, the dead:
Talk'd much of *Satan* and the land of woe,
And many a chapter from the scriptures read.

At last he rais'd the swelling anthem high;
In dismal numbers seem'd he to complain:
The captive tribes that by *Euphrates* wept,
Their song was jovial to his dreary strain.

That done, they plac'd the carcase in the tomb,
To dust and dull oblivion now resign'd;
Then turn'd the chariot tow'rd the House of Night,
Which soon flew off and left no trace behind.

But as I stoop'd to write the appointed verse,
Swifter than thought the airy scene decay'd;
Blushing the morn arose, and from the east
With her gay streams of light dispell'd the shade.

The Beauties of Santa Cruz, selections [*1776*]

From the vast caverns of old ocean's bed,
Fair Santa Cruz, arising, laves her waist,
The threatening waters roar on every side,
For every side by ocean is embraced.

Sharp, craggy rocks repel the surging brine,
Whose caverned sides by restless billows wore,
Resemblance claim to that remoter isle
Where once the winds' proud lord the sceptre bore.

Betwixt old Cancer and the midway line,
In happiest climate lies this envied isle,
Trees bloom throughout the year, streams ever flow,
And fragrant Flora wears a lasting smile.

Cool, woodland streams from shaded clifts descend,
The dripping rock no want of moisture knows,
Supplied by springs that on the skies depend,
That fountain feeding as the current flows.

Such were the isles which happy Flaccus sung,
Where one tree blossoms while another bears,
Where Spring forever gay, and ever young,
Walks her gay round through her unwearied years.

Such were the climes which youthful Eden saw
Ere crossing fates destroyed her golden reign—
Reflect upon thy loss, unhappy man,
And seek the vales of Paradise again.

George The Third's Soliloquy [1779]

What mean these dreams, and hideous forms that rise
Night after night, tormenting to my eyes—
No real foes these horrid shapes can be,
But thrice as much they vex and torture me.
    How cursed is he,—how doubly cursed am I—
Who lives in pain, and yet who dares not die;
To him no joy this world of Nature brings,
In vain the wild rose blooms, the daisy springs.
Is this a prelude to some new disgrace,
Some baleful omen to my name and race!—
It may be so—ere mighty Cæsar died
Presaging Nature felt his doom, and sighed;
A bellowing voice through midnight groves was heard,

And threatening ghosts at dusk of eve appeared—
Ere Brutus fell, to adverse fates a prey,
His evil genius met him on the way,
And so may mine!—but who would yield so soon
A prize, some luckier hour may make my own?
Shame seize my crown, ere such a deed be mine—
No—to the last my squadrons shall combine,
And slay my foes, while foes remain to slay,
Or *heaven* shall grant me one successful day.
    Is there a robber close in Newgate hemmed,
Is there a cut-throat, fettered and condemned?
Haste, loyal slaves, to George's standard come,
Attend his lectures when you hear the drum;
Your chains I break—for better days prepare,
Come out, my friends, from prison and from care,
Far to the west I plan your desperate sway,
There, 'tis no sin to ravage, burn, and slay
There, without fear, your bloody aims pursue,
And shew mankind what English thieves can do.
    That day, when first I mounted to the throne,
I swore to let all foreign foes alone.
Through love of peace to terms did I advance,
And made, they say, a shameful league with France.
But different scenes rise horrid to my view,
I charged my hosts to plunder and subdue—
At first, indeed, I thought short wars to wage
And sent some jail-birds to be led by *Gage*.
For 'twas but right, that those we marked for slaves
Should be reduced by cowards, fools, and knaves;
Awhile, directed by his feeble hand,
Those *troops* were kicked and pelted through the land,
Or starved in Boston, cursed the unlucky hour
They left their dungeons for that fatal shore.
    France aids them now, a desperate game I play,
And hostile Spain will do the same, they say;
My armies vanquished, and my heroes fled,
My people murmuring, and my commerce dead,
My shattered navy pelted, bruised, and clubbed,

By Dutchmen bullied, and by Frenchmen drubbed,
My name abhorred, my nation in disgrace,
,How should I act in such a mournful case!
My hopes and joys are vanished with my coin,
My ruined army, and my lost Burgoyne!
What shall I do—confess my labours vain,
Or whet my tusks, and to the charge again!
But where's my force—my choicest troops are fled,
Some thousands crippled, and a myriad dead—
If I were owned the boldest of mankind,
And hell with all her flames inspired my mind,
Could I at once with Spain and France contend,
And fight the *rebels*, on the world's green end?—
The pangs of *parting* I can ne'er endure,
Yet *part* we must, and part to meet no more!
Oh, blast the *Congress*, blast each upstart state,
On whose commands ten thousand captains wait;
From various climes that dire *Assembly* came,
True to their trust, as hostile to my fame;
'Tis these, ah these, have ruined half my sway,
Disgraced my arms, and led my slaves astray—
Cursed be the day, when first I saw the sun,
Cursed be the hour, when I these wars begun:
The fiends of darkness then possessed my mind,
And powers unfriendly to the human kind.
To wasting grief, and sullen rage a prey,
To *Scotland's* utmost verge I'll take my way,
There with eternal storms due concert keep,
And while the billows rage, as fiercely weep—
Ye highland lads, my rugged fate bemoan,
Assist me with one sympathizing groan;
For late I find the nations are my foes,
I must submit, and that with bloody nose,
Or, like our James, fly basely from the state,
Or share, what still is worse—old *Charles's* fate.

The British Prison Ship, Canto III [*1780*]

[The Hospital Prison Ship]

Now toward the *Hunter's* gloomy sides we came,
A slaughter-house, yet hospital in name;
For none came there (to pass through all degrees)
Till half consumed, and dying with disease;—
But when too near with laboring oars we plied,
The Mate with curses drove us from the side;
That wretch who, banished from the navy crew,
Grown old in blood, did here his trade renew;
His serpent's tongue, when on his charge let loose,
Uttered reproaches, scandal, and abuse,
Gave all to hell who dared his king disown,
And swore mankind were made for George alone:
Ten thousand times, to irritate our woe,
He wished us foundered in the gulf below;
Ten thousand times he brandished high his stick,
And swore as often that we were not sick—
And yet so pale!—that we were thought by some
A freight of ghosts from Death's dominions come—
But calmed at length—for who can always rage,
Or the fierce war of endless passion wage?—
He pointed to the stairs that led below
To damps, disease, and varied shapes of woe.
Down to the gloom I took my pensive way,
Along the decks the dying captives lay;
Some struck with madness, some with scurvy pained,
But still of putrid fevers most complained!
On the hard floors these wasted objects laid,
There tossed and tumbled in the dismal shade,
There no soft voice their bitter fate bemoaned,
And Death strode stately, while the victims groaned;
Of leaky decks I heard them long complain,
Drowned as they were in deluges of rain,
Denied the comforts of a dying bed,
And not a pillow to support the head—

How could they else but pine, and grieve, and sigh,
Detest a wretched life—and wish to die?
Scarce had I mingled with this dismal band
When a thin spectre seized me by the hand—
"And art thou come (death heavy on his eyes),
And art thou come to these abodes?" he cries;
"Why didst thou leave *Scorpion's* dark retreat,
And hither haste a surer death to meet?
Why didst thou leave thy damp infected cell?
If that was purgatory, this is hell—
We, too, grown weary of that horrid shade,
Petitioned early for the doctor's aid;
His aid denied, more deadly symptoms came,
Weak, and yet weaker, glowed the vital flame;
And when disease had worn us down so low
That few could tell if we were ghosts or no,
And all asserted, death would be our fate—
Then to the doctor we were sent—too late.
Here wastes away Autolycus the brave,
Here young Orestes finds a watery grave,
Here gay Alcander, gay, alas! no more,
Dies far sequestered from his native shore;
He late, perhaps, too eager for the fray,
Chased the vile Briton o'er the watery way
Till fortune, jealous, bade her clouds appear,
Turned hostile to his fame, and brought him here.
"Thus do our warriors, thus our heroes fall,
Imprisoned here, base ruin meets them all,
Or, sent afar to Britain's barbarous shore,
There die neglected, and return no more:
Ah! rest in peace, poor, injured, parted shade,
By cruel hands in death's dark weeds arrayed,
But happier climes, where suns unclouded shine,
Light undisturbed, and endless peace are thine."—
From Brookland groves a Hessian doctor came,
Nor great his skill, nor greater much his fame;
Fair Science never called the wretch her son,
And Art disdained the stupid man to own;—
Can you admire that Science was so coy,

Or Art refused his genius to employ!—
Do men with brutes an equal dullness share,
Or cuts yon grovelling mole the midway air?
In polar worlds can Eden's blossoms blow?
Do trees of God in barren deserts grow?
Are loaded vines to Etna's summit known,
Or swells the peach beneath the torrid zone?—
Yet still he doomed his genius to the rack,
And, as you may suppose, was owned a quack.

*To the Memory of the Brave Americans, Under General Greene,
in South Carolina, Who fell in the Action of September 8, 1781*
[*1781*]

At Eutaw springs the valiant died:
Their limbs with dust are covered o'er—
Weep on, ye springs, your tearful tide;
How many heroes are no more!

If in this wreck of ruin, they
Can yet be thought to claim a tear,
O smite your gentle breast, and say
The friends of freedom slumber here!

Thou who shalt trace this bloody plain,
If goodness rules thy generous breast,
Sigh for the wasted rural reign;
Sigh for the shepherds, sunk to rest!

Stranger, their humble graves adorn;
You too may fall, and ask a tear:
'Tis not the beauty of the morn
That proves the evening shall be clear—

They saw their injured country's woe;
The flaming town, the wasted field;
Then rushed to meet the insulting foe;
They took the spear—but left the shield.

Led by thy conquering genius, Greene,
The Britons they compelled to fly:
None distant viewed the fatal plain,
None grieved, in such a cause to die—

But, like the Parthian, famed of old,
Who, flying, still their arrows threw;
These routed Britons, full as bold,
Retreated, and retreating slew.

Now rest in peace, our patriot band;
Though far from Nature's limits thrown,
We trust, they find a happier land,
A brighter sun-shine of their own.

On The Memorable Victory [1781]

Obtained by the Gallant Captain Paul Jones, of the "Good Man
Richard" over the "Seraphis," Etc., under the Command of
Captain Pearson.

O'er the rough main with flowing sheet
The guardian of a numerous fleet,
    Seraphis from the Baltic came;
A ship of less tremendous force
Sailed by her side the self-same course,
    Countess of Scarb'ro' was her name.

And now their native coasts appear,
Britannia's hills their summits rear
   Above the German main;
Fond to suppose their dangers o'er,
They southward coast along the shore,
   Thy waters, gentle Thames, to gain.

Full forty guns *Seraphis* bore,
And *Scarb'ro's Countess* twenty-four,
   Manned with Old England's boldest tars—
What flag that rides the Gallic seas
Shall dare attack such piles as these,
   Designed for tumults and for wars!

Now from the top-mast's giddy height
A seaman cried—"Four sails in sight
   Approach with favoring gales";
Pearson, resolved to save the fleet,
Stood off to sea these ships to meet,
   And closely braced his shivering sails.

With him advanced the *Countess* bold,
Like a black tar in wars grown old:
   And now these floating piles drew nigh;
But, muse, unfold what chief of fame
In th' other warlike squadron came,
   Whose standards at his masthead fly.

'Twas Jones, brave Jones, to battle led
As bold a crew as ever bled
   Upon the sky surrounded main;
The standards of the Western World
Were to the willing winds unfurled,
   Denying Britain's tyrant reigh.

The *Good Man Richard* led the line;
The *Alliance* next: with these combine

The Gallic ship they *Pallas* call:
The *Vengeance*, armed with sword and flame,
These to attack the Britons came—
    But two accomplished all.

Now Phœbus sought his pearly bed:
But who can tell the scenes of dread,
    The horrors of that fatal night!
Close us these floating castles came;
The *Good Man Richard* bursts in flame;
    Seraphis trembled at the sight.

She felt the fury of her ball,
Down, prostrate down, the Britons fall;
    The decks were strewed with slain:
Jones to the foe his vessel lashed;
And, while the black artillery flashed,
    Loud thunders shook the main.

Alas! that mortals should employ
Such murdering engines, to destroy
    That frame by heaven so nicely joined;
Alas! that e'er the God decreed
That brother should by brother bleed,
    And poured such madness in the mind.

But thou, brave Jones, no blame shalt bear;
The rights of men demand thy care:
    For these you dare the greedy waves—
No tyrant on destruction bent
Has planned thy conquests—thou art sent
    To humble tyrants and their slaves.

See!—dread *Seraphis* flames again—
And art thou, Jones, among the slain,
    And sunk to Neptune's caves below?
He lives—though crowds around him fall,
Still he, unhurt, survives them all;
    Almost alone he fights the foe.

And can thy ship these strokes sustain?
Behold thy brave companions slain,
   All clasped in ocean's dark embrace.
"Strike, or be sunk!"—the Briton cries—
"Sink, if you can!"—the chief replies,
   Fierce lightnings blazing in his face.

Then to the side three guns he drew
(Almost deserted by his crew)
   And charged them deep with woe:
By Pearson's flash he aimed the balls;
His main-mast totters—down it falls—
   Tremendous was the blow.

Pearson as yet disdained to yield,
But scarce his secret fears concealed,
   And thus was heard to cry—
"With hell, not mortals, I contend;
What art thou—human, or a fiend,
   That dost my force defy?

"Return, my lads, the fight renew!"
So called bold Pearson to his crew;
   But called, alas! in vain;
Some on the decks lay maimed and dead;
Some to their deep recesses fled,
   And more were buried in the main.

Distressed, forsaken, and alone,
He hauled his tattered standard down,
   And yielded to his gallant foe;
Bold *Pallas* soon the *Countess* took,
Thus both their haughty colors struck,
   Confessing what the brave can do.

But, Jones, too dearly didst thou buy
These ships possess so gloriously,
   Too many deaths disgraced the fray:
Thy barque that bore the conquering flame,
That the proud Briton overcame,
   Even she forsook thee on thy way;

For when the morn began to shine,
Fatal to her, the ocean brine
   Poured through each spacious wound;
Quick in the deep she disappeared,
But Jones to friendly Belgia steered,
   With conquest and with glory crowned.

Go on, great man, to daunt the foe,
And bid the haughty Britons know
   They to our Thirteen Stars shall bend;
The Stars that veiled in dark attire,
Long glimmered with a feeble fire,
   But radiant now ascend;

Bend to the Stars that flaming rise
In western, not in eastern, skies,
   Fair Freedom's reign restored.
So when the Magi, come from far,
Beheld the God-attending Star,
   They trembled and adored.

The Political Balance, selections [*1782*]

As Jove the Olympian (who both I and you know
Was brother to Neptune and husband to Juno)
Was lately reviewing his papers of state,
He happened to light on the records of Fate.

In Alphabet order this volume was written,
So he opened at B, for the article "Britain":
"She struggles so well," said the god, "I will see
What the sisters in Pluto's dominions decree."

At first on the top of a column he read
"Of a king with a mighty soft place in his head,
Who should join in his temper the ass and the mule,
The third of his name, and by far the worst fool.".…

So Jupiter read, a god of first rank,
And still had read on, but he came to a blank:
For the Fates had neglected the rest to reveal—
They either forgot it, or chose to conceal.

When a leaf is torn out, or a blot on a page
That pleases our fancy, we fly in a rage;
So, curious to know what the Fates would say next,
No wonder if Jove, disappointed, was vext.

But still, as true genius not frequently fails,
He glanced at the *Virgin*, and thought of the *Scales*.
And said, "To determine the will of the Fates,
One scale shall weigh *Britain*, the other the *States*."

Then turning to Vulcan, his maker of thunder,
Said he, "My dear Vulcan, I pray you look yonder:
Those *creatures* are tearing each other to pieces,
And instead of abating the carnage increases.

"Now as you are a blacksmith, and lusty stout ham-eater,
You must make me a globe of a shorter diameter—
The world in abridgement and just as it stands,
With all its proportions of water and lands.

"But its various divisions must so be designed
That I can unhinge it whene'er I've a mind—
How else should I know what the portions will weigh,
Or which of the combatants carry the day?"

Old Vulcan complied (we've no reason to doubt it),
So he put on his apron and strait went about it;
Made center, and circles as round as a pancake,
And here the Pacific and there the Atlantic.....

At length, to discourage all stupid pretensions,
Jove looked at the globe and approved its dimensions,
And cried in a transport, "Why, what have we here?
Friend Vulcan, it is a most beautiful sphere!

"Now while I am busy in taking apart
This globe that is formed with such exquisite art,
Go, Hermes, to Libra (you're one of her gallants),
And ask in my name for the loan of her balance."

Away posted Hermes, as swift as the gales,
And as swiftly returned with the ponderous scales;
And hung them aloft to a beam in the air,
So equally poised they had turned with a hair.

Now Jove to Columbia his shoulders applied;
But, aiming to lift her, his strength she defied:
Then, turning about to their godships, he says,
"A body so vast is not easy to raise;

"But if you assist me, I still have a *notion*
Our *forces united* can put her in motion
And swing her aloft, though alone I might fail,
And place her, in spite of her bulk, in our scale.

"If six years together the Congress have strove,
And more than *divided the empire with Jove,*
With a Jove like myself, who am *nine* times as great,
You can join, like their soldiers, to heave up this weight."

So to it they went, with handspikes and levers,
And upward she sprung, with her mountains and rivers,
Rocks, cities, and islands, deep waters and shallows,
Ships, armies, and forests, high heads and fine fellows.....

Then, searching about with his fingers for Britain,
Thought he, "This same island I cannot well hit on;
The devil take him who first called her the Great—
If she was, she is *vastly* diminished of late."

Like a man that is searching his thigh for a flea,
He peeped and he fumbled, but nothing could see.
At last he exclaimed, "I am surely upon it—
I think I have hold of a Highlander's bonnet."

But finding his error, he said with a sigh,
"This bonnet is only the island of Skie!"
So away to his *namesake* the Planet he goes,
And borrowed *two moons* to hang on his nose.

Through these, as through glasses, he saw her quite clear,
And in raptures cried out, "I have found her—she's here!
If this be not Britain, then call me an ass—
She *looks like a gem in an ocean of glass.*"....

Then he raised her aloft; but—to shorten our tale—
She looked like a clod in the opposite scale;
Britannia so small, and Columbia so large—
A ship of first rate, and a ferryman's barge.

Cried Pallas to Vulcan, "Why, Jove's in a dream.
Observe how he watches the turn of the beam!
Was ever a mountain outweighed by a grain?
Or what is a drop when compared to the main?"

But Momus alleged, "In my humble opinion,
You should add to Great-Britain her foreign dominion:
When this is appended, perhaps she will rise,
And equal her rival in weight and in size."

"Alas," said the monarch, "your project is vain:
But little is left of her foreign domain;
And, scattered about in the liquid expanse,
That little is left to the mercy of France.

"However, we'll lift them, and give her fair play."
And soon in the scale with their mistress they lay;
But the gods were confounded and struck with surprise,
And Vulcan could hardly believe his own eyes:

For, such was the purpose and guidance of fate,
Her foreign dominions diminished her weight;
By which it appeared, to Britain's disaster,
Her foreign possessions were changing their master.

Then, as he replaced them, said Jove with a smile,
"Columbia shall never be ruled by an isle;
But vapours and darkness around her may rise,
And tempests conceal her a-while from our eyes.

"So locusts in Egypt their squadrons display,
And, rising, disfigure the face of the day;
So the moon, at her full, has a frequent eclipse,
And the sun in the ocean diurnally dips.

"Then cease your endeavours, ye vermin of Britain"
(And here in derision their island he spit on):
"'Tis madness to seek what you never can find,
Or to think of uniting what Nature disjoined.

"But still you may flutter awhile with your wings,
And spit out your venom and brandish your stings:
Your hearts are as black and as bitter as gall,
A curse to mankind, and a blot on the Ball."

On Retirement [1786]

A hermit's house beside a stream
    With forests planted round,
Whatever it to you may seem
More real happiness I deem
    Than if I were a monarch crowned.

A cottage I could call my own
    Remote from domes of care;
A little garden, walled with stone,
The wall with ivy overgrown,
    A limpid fountain near,

Would more substantial joys afford,
    More real bliss impart
Than all the wealth that misers hoard,
Than vanquished worlds, or worlds restored—
    Mere cankers of the heart!

Vain, foolish man! how vast thy pride,
    How little can your wants supply!—
'Tis surely wrong to grasp so wide—
You act as if you only had
    To triumph—not to die!

The Wild Honey Suckle [1786]

Fair flower, that dost so comely grow,
Hid in this silent, dull retreat,
Untouched thy honied blossoms blow,
Unseen thy little branches greet:
    No roving foot shall crush thee here,
    No busy hand provoke a tear.

By Nature's self in white arrayed,
She bade thee shun the vulgar eye,
And planted here the guardian shade,
And sent soft waters murmuring by;
    Thus quietly thy summer goes,
    Thy days declining to repose,

Smit with those charms, that must decay,
I grieve to see your future doom;
They died—nor were those flowers more gay,
The flowers that did in Eden bloom;
    Unpitying frosts, and Autumn's power
    Shall leave no vestige of this flower.

From morning suns and evening dews
At first thy little being came:
If nothing once, you nothing lose,
For when you die you are the same;
    The space between, is but an hour,
    The frail duration of a flower.

The Indian Burying Ground [1787]

In spite of all the learned have said,
I still my old opinion keep;
The *posture*, that *we* give the dead,
Points out the soul's eternal sleep.

Not so the ancients of these lands—
The Indian, when from life released,
Again is seated with his friends,
And shares again the joyous feast.

His imaged birds, and painted bowl,
And venison, for a journey dressed,
Bespeak the nature of the soul,
Activity, that knows no rest.

His bow, for action ready bent,
And arrows, with a head of stone,
Can only mean that life is spent,
And not the old ideas gone.

Thou, stranger, that shalt come this way,
No fraud upon the dead commit—
Observe the swelling turf, and say
They do not *lie*, but here they *sit*.

Here still a lofty rock remains,
On which the curious eye may trace
(Now wasted, half, by wearing rains)
The fancies of a ruder race.

Here still an aged elm aspires,
Beneath whose far-projecting shade
(And which the shepherd still admires)
The children of the forest played!

There oft a restless Indian queen
(Pale *Shebah*, with her braided hair)
And many a barbarous form is seen
To chide the man that lingers there.

By midnight moons, o'er moistening dews,
In habit for the chase arrayed,
The hunter still the deer pursues,
The hunter and the deer, a shade!

And long shall timorous fancy see
The painted chief, and pointed spear,
And Reason's self shall bow the knee
To shadows and delusions here.

To An Author [1788]

Your leaves bound up compact and fair,
In neat array at length prepare,
To pass their hour on learning's stage,
To meet the surly critic's rage;
The statesman's slight, the smatterer's sneer—
Were these, indeed, your only fear,
You might be tranquil and resigned:
What most should touch your fluttering mind;
Is that, few critics will be found
To sift your works, and deal the wound.

Thus, when one fleeting year is past
On some bye-shelf *your* book is cast—
Another comes, with *something new,*
And drives you fairly out of view:

With some to praise, *but more to blame,*
The mind returns to—whence it came;
And some alive, who *scarce could read*
Will publish satires on the dead.

Thrice happy Dryden, who could meet
Some rival bard in every street!
When all were bent on writing well
It was some credit to excel:—

Thrice happy Dryden, who could find
A *Milbourne* for his sport designed—
And *Pope*, who saw the harmless rage
Of *Dennis* bursting o'er his page
Might justly sprun the *critic's aim,*
Who only helped to swell his fame.

On these bleak climes by Fortune thrown,
Where rigid *Reason* reigns alone,
Where lovely *Fancy* has no sway,
Nor magic forms about us play—
Nor nature takes her summer hue
Tell me, what has the muse to do?—

An age employed in edging steel
Can no poetic raptures feel;
No solitude's attracting power,
No leisure of the noon day hour,
No shaded stream, no quiet grove
Can this fantastic century move,

The muse of love in no request—
Go—try your fortune with the rest,
One of the nine you should engage,
To meet the follies of the age:—

On *one*, we fear, your choice must fall—
The least engaging of them all—
Her visage stern—an angry style—
A clouded brow—malicious smile—
A mind on *murdered victims* placed—
She, only she, can please the taste!

The Indian Student [*1788*]

From Susquehanna's farthest springs,
Where savage tribes pursue their game,
(His blanket tied with yellow strings,)
A shepherd of the forest came.

Not long before, a wandering priest
Express'd his wish with visage sad—
"Ah, why (he cried) in Satan's waste,
Ah, why detain so fine a lad?

"In white man's land there stands a town,
Where learning may be purchased low—
Exchange his blanket for a gown,
And let the lad to college go."

From long debate the council rose,
And viewing Shalum's tricks with joy,
To Cambridge Hall, o'er wastes of snows,
They sent the copper-color'd boy.

One generous chief a bow supplied,
This gave a shaft, and that a skin;
The feathers, in vermilion dyed,
Himself did from a turkey win:

Thus dress'd so gay, he took his way
O'er barren hills, alone, alone!
His guide a star, he wander'd far,
His pillow every night a stone.

At last he came, with foot so lame,
Where learned men talk heathen Greek,
And Hebrew lore is gabbled o'er,
To please the muses,—twice a week.

Awhile he writ, awhile he read,
Awhile he conn'd their grammar rules—
(An Indian savage so well bred
Great credit promised to the schools.)

Some thought he would in law excel,
Some said in physic he would shine;
And one that knew him passing well,
Beheld in him a sound divine.

But those of more discerning eye,
Even then could other prospects show,
And saw him lay his Virgil by,
To wander with his dearer bow.

The tedious hours of study spent,
The heavy moulded lecture done,
He to the woods a hunting went,
Through lonely wastes he walk'd, he run.

No mystic wonders fired his mind;
He sought to gain no learn'd degree,
But only sense enough to find
The squirrel in the hollow tree.

The shady bank, the purling stream,
The woody wild his heart possess'd,
The dewy lawn, his morning dream
In fancy's gayest colors drest.

"And why," he cried, "did I forsake
My native wood for gloomy walls;
The silver stream, the limpid lake
For musty books, and college halls.

"A little could my wants supply—
Can wealth and honor give me more;
Or, will the sylvan god deny
The humble treat he gave before?

"Let seraphs gain the bright abode,
And heaven's sublimest mansions see—
I only bow to Nature's God—
The land of shades will do for me.

"These dreadful secrets of the sky
Alarm my soul with chilling fear—
Do planets in their orbits fly,
And is the earth, indeed, a sphere?

"Let planets still their course pursue,
And comets to the centre run—
In him my faithful friend I view,
The image of my God—the sun.

"Where nature's ancient forests grow,
And mingled laurel never fades,
My heart is fix'd and I must go
To die among my native shades."

He spoke, and to the western springs,
(His gown discharged, his money spent,
His blanket with yellow strings,)
The shepherd of the forest went.

On Mr. Paine's Rights of Man [1791]

Thus briefly sketched the sacred Rights of Man,
How inconsistent with the Royal Plan!
Which for itself exclusive honour craves,
Where some are masters born, and millions slaves.
With what contempt must every eye look down
On that base, childish bauble called a *crown*,
The gilded bait, that lures the crowd, to come,
Bow down their necks, and meet a slavish doom;
The source of half the miseries men endure,
The quack that kills them, while it seems to cure.
    Roused by the Reason of his manly page,
Once more shall Paine a listening world engage:
From Reason's source, a bold reform he brings,
In raising up mankind, he pulls down *kings,*
Who, source of discord, patrons of all wrong,
On blood and murder have been fed too long:
Hid from the world, and tutored to be base,
The curse, the scourge, the ruin of our race,

Their's was the task, a full designing few,
To shackle beings that they scarcely knew,
Who made this globe the residence of slaves,
And built their thrones on systems formed by knaves
—Advance, bright years, to work their final fall,
And haste the period that shall crush them all.
Who, that has read and scann'd the historic page
But glows, at every line, with kindling rage,
To see by them the rights of men aspersed,
Freedom restrain'd, and Nature's law reversed,
Man, ranked with beasts, by monarchs *will'd* away,
And bound young fools, or madmen to obey:
Now driven to wars, and now oppressed at home,
Compelled in crowds o'er distant seas to roam,
From India's climes the plundered prize to bring
To glad the strumpet, or to glut the king.
Columbia, hail! immortal be thy reign:
Without a king, we till the smiling plain;
Without a king, we traced the unbounded sea,
And traffic round the globe, through each degree;
Each foreign clime our honour'd flag reveres,
Which asks no monarch, to support the Stars:
Without a *king*, the laws maintain their sway,
While honour bids each generous heart obey.
Be ours the task the ambitious to restrain,
And this great lesson teach—that kings are vain;
That warring realms to certain ruin haste,
That kings subsist by war, and wars are waste:
So shall our nation, form'd on Virtue's plan,
Remain the guardian of the Rights of Man,
A vast Republic, famed through every clime,
Without a king, to see the end of time.

To the Americans of the United States [1797]

Men of this passing age!—whose noble deeds
Honour will bear above the *scum* of Time:
Ere this eventful century expire,
Once more we greet you with our humble rhyme:
Pleased, if we meet your smiles, but—if denied,
Yet, with YOUR sentence, we are satisfied.

Catching our subjects from the varying scene
Of human things: a mingled work we draw,
Chequered with fancies odd, and figures strange,
Such, as no *courtly* poet ever saw;
Who writ, beneath some Great Man's ceiling placed;
Travelled no lands, nor roved the watery waste.

To seize some *features* from the faithless past;
Be this our care—before the century close:
The colours strong!—for, if we deem aright,
The *coming age will be an age of prose:*
When *sordid cares* will break the muses' dream,
And Common Sense be ranked in seat supreme,

Go, now, dear book; once more expand your wings:
Still to the cause of Man *severely true:*
Untaught to flatter *pride,* or fawn on kings;—
Trojan, or Tyrian,—*give them both their due.—*
When they are right, the cause of both we plead,
And both will please us well,—if both will read.

TIMOTHY DWIGHT [1752-1817]

Having shown great precocity as a child, Timothy Dwight was encouraged by his prominent New England family (he was a grandson of Jonathan Edwards) in his scholarly pursuits. A graduate of Yale, and later a most distinguished president of that institution, Dwight possessed great literary ambitions while an undergraduate.

A member of the Connecticut Wits, his most popular work during the Revolution was "Columbia," a war song credited with great inspirational value among the soldiers, which he wrote while serving as an army chaplain.

"Greenfield Hills," which he wrote while taking long daily walks when he was a pastor in Greenfield, Connecticut, survives as perhaps his best poetical effort.

Columbia [*1777*]

Columbia, Columbia, to glory arise,
The queen of the world, and the child of the skies!
Thy genius commands thee; with rapture behold,
While ages on ages thy splendors unfold.
Thy reign is the last, and the noblest of time,
Most fruitful thy soil, most inviting thy clime;
Let the crimes of the east ne'er encrimson thy name,
Be freedom, and science, and virtue thy fame.

To conquest and slaughter let Europe aspire;
Whelm nations in blood, and wrap cities in fire;
Thy heroes the rights of mankind shall defend,
And triumph pursue them, and glory attend.
A world is thy realm: for a world be thy laws,
Enlarged as thine empire, and just as thy cause;
On freedom's broad basis, that empire shall rise,
Extend with the main, and dissolve with the skies.

Fair Science her gates to thy sons shall unbar,
And the east see thy morn hide the beams of her star.
New bards, and new sages, unrivall'd shall soar
To fame unextinguish'd, when time is no more;
To thee, the last refuge of virtue designed,
Shall fly from all nations the best of mankind;
Here, grateful to heaven, with transport shall bring
Their incense, more fragrant than odors of spring.

Nor less shall thy fair ones to glory ascend,
And genius and beauty in harmony blend;
The graces of form shall awake pure desire,
And the charms of the soul ever cherish the fire;
Their sweetness unmingled, their manners refined,
And virtue's bright image, instamp'd on the mind,
With peace, and soft rapture, shall teach life to glow,
And light up a smile in the aspect of woe.

Thy fleets to all regions thy power shall display,
The nations admire, and the ocean obey;
Each shore to thy glory its tribute unfold,
And the east and the south yield their spices and gold.
As the day-spring unbounded, thy splendor shall flow,
And earth's little kingdoms before thee shall bow:
While the ensigns of union, in triumph unfurl'd,
Hush the tumult of war, and give peace to the world.

Thus, as down a lone valley, with cedars o'erspread,
From war's dread confusion I pensively stray'd—
The gloom from the face of fair heaven retired;
The winds ceased to murmur; the thunders expired;
Perfumes, as of Eden, flow'd sweetly along,
And a voice, as of angels, enchantingly sung:
"Columbia, Columbia, to glory arise,
The queen of the world and the child of the skies."

Greenfield Hill, selections [*1794*]

Part II

Fair Verna, loveliest village of the west,
Of every joy and every charm possess'd,
How pleas'd amid thy varied walks I rove,
Sweet, cheerful walks of innocence and love,
And o'er thy smiling prospects cast my eyes
And see the seats of peace and pleasure rise,
And hear the voice of Industry resound,
And mark the smile of Competence around.
Hail, happy village! O'er thy cheerful lawns,
With earliest beauty, spring delighted dawns:
The northward sun begins his vernal smile,
The spring-bird carols o'er the cressy rill;
The shower that patters in the ruffled stream,

The ploughboy's voice that chides the lingering team,
The bee, industrious, with his busy song,
The woodman's axe the distant groves among,
The waggon rattling down the rugged steep,
The light wind lulling every care to sleep,
All these, with mingled music, from below
Deceive intruding sorrow as I go.
    How pleas'd fond Recollection, with a smile,
Surveys the varied round of wintery toil;
How pleas'd, amid the flowers that scent the plain,
Recalls the vanish'd frost and sleeted rain,
The chilling damp, the ice-endangering street,
And treacherous earth that slump'd beneath the feet.
    Yet even stern winter's glooms could joy inspire:
Then social circles grac'd the nutwood fire;
The axe resounded at the sunny door;
The swain, industrious, trimm'd his flaxen store,
Or thresh'd, with vigorous flail, the bounding wheat,
His poultry round him pilfering for their meat,
Or slid his firewood on the creaking snow,
Or bore his produce to the main below,
Or o'er his rich returns exulting laugh'd,
Or pledg'd the healthful orchard's sparkling draught;
While, on his board for friends and neighbours spread,
The turkey smoak'd his busy housewife fed,
And Hospitality look'd smiling round,
And Leisure told his tale with gleeful sound.....
    But now the wintery glooms are vanish'd all:
The lingering drift behind the shady wall,
The dark-brown spots that patch'd the snowy field,
The surly frost that every bud conceal'd,
The russet veil, the way with slime o'erspread,
And all the saddening scenes of March are fled.
    Sweet-smiling village, loveliest of the hills,
How green thy groves, how pure thy glassy rills!
With what new joy I walk thy verdant streets,
How often pause to breathe thy gale of sweets,
To mark thy well-built walls, thy budding fields,

And every charm that rural nature yields,
And every joy to Competence allied,
And every good that Virtue gains from Pride.
No griping landlord here alarms the door,
To halve for rent the poor man's little store.
No haughty owner drives the humble swain
To some far refuge from his dread domain,
Nor wastes upon his robe of useless pride
The wealth which shivering thousands want beside,
Nor in one palace sinks a hundred cots,
Nor in one manor drowns a thousand lots,
Nor on one table, spread for death and pain,
Devours what would a village well sustain.....
    Beside yon church that beams a modest ray,
With tidy neatness reputable gay,
When, mild and fair as Eden's seventh-day light,
In silver silence shines the Sabbath bright,
In neat attire the village households come
And learn the path-way to the eternal home.
Hail, solemn ordinance worthy of the Skies,
Whence thousand richest blessings daily rise:
Peace, order, cleanliness, and manners sweet,
A sober mind, to rule submission meet,
Enlarging knowledge, life from guilt refin'd,
And love to God, and friendship to mankind.
In the clear splendour of thy vernal morn,
New-quicken'd man to light and life is born;
The desert of the mind with virtue blooms,
Its flowers unfold, its fruits exhale perfumes;
Proud guilt dissolves beneath the searching ray,
And low debasement trembling creeps away;
Vice bites the dust, foul Error seeks her den,
And God descending dwells anew with men.
    Where yonder humbler spire salutes the eye,
Its vane slow turning in the liquid sky,
Where in light gambols healthy striplings sport,
Ambitious learning builds her outer court.
A grave preceptor there her usher stands,

And rules without a rod her little bands.
Some half-grown sprigs of learning grac'd his brow:
Little he knew, though much he wish'd to know;
Inchanted hung o'er Virgil's honey'd lay,
And smil'd to see desipient Horace play;
Glean'd scraps of Greek, and, curious, trac'd afar
Through Pope's clear glass the bright Mæonian star.
Yet oft his students at his wisdom star'd,
For many a student to his side repair'd;
Surpriz'd they heard him Dilworth's knots untie,
And tell what lands beyond the Atlantic lie.
Many his faults, his virtues small and few;
Some little good he did or strove to do:
Laborious still, he taught the early mind,
And urg'd to manners meek and thoughts refin'd;
Truth he impress'd, and every virtue prais'd,
While infant eyes in wondering silence gaz'd;
The worth of time would day by day unfold,
And tell them every hour was made of gold;
Brown Industry he lov'd, and oft declar'd
How hardy Sloth in life's sad evening far'd.

Part IV

Ah me, while up the long, long vale of time
Reflection wanders towards th' eternal vast,
How starts the eye at many a change sublime,
Unbosom'd dimly by the ages pass'd.
What Mausoleums crowd the mournful waste,
The tombs of empires fallen and nations gone:
Each, once inscrib'd in gold with "Aye to last,"
Sate as a queen, proclaim'd the world her own,
And proudly cried, "By me no sorrows shall be known."

Soon fleets the sunbright Form by man ador'd:
Soon fell the Head of gold, to Time a prey;
The Arms, the Trunk his cankering tooth devour'd,
And whirlwinds blew the Iron dust away.

Where dwelt imperia! Timur?—far astray
Some lonely-musing pilgrim now enquires;
And, rack'd by storms and hastening to decay,
Mohammed's Mosque forsees it's final fires;
And Rome's more lordly Temple day by day expires.

As o'er proud Asian realms the traveller winds,
His manly spirit hush'd by terror falls,
When some deceased town's lost site he finds,
Where ruin wild his pondering eye appals,
Where silence swims along the moulder'd walls
And broods upon departed Grandeur's tomb.
Through the lone hollow aisles sad Echo calls,
At each slow step; deep sighs the breathing gloom,
And weeping fields around bewail their Empress' doom.

Where o'er an hundred realms the throne uprose,
The screech-owl nests, the panther builds his home;
Sleep the dull newts, the lazy adders doze,
Where pomp and luxury danc'd the golden room.
Low lies in dust the sky-resembled dome;
Tall grass around the broken column waves;
And brambles climb and lonely thistles bloom;
The moulder'd arch the weedy streamlet laves,
And low resound, beneath, unnumber'd sunken graves.

Soon fleets the sun-bright Form by man ador'd,
And soon man's dæmon chiefs from memory fade.
In musty volume now must be explor'd
Where dwelt imperial nations long decay'd.
The brightest meteors angry clouds invade,
And where the wonders glitter'd none explain.
Where Carthage with proud hand the trident sway'd,
Now mud-wall'd cots sit sullen on the plain,
And wandering, fierce, and wild, sequester'd Arabs reign.

In thee, O Albion, queen of nations, live
Whatever splendours earth's wide realms have known:
In thee proud Persia sees her pomp revive,
And Greece her arts, and Rome her lordly throne;
By every wind thy Tyrian fleets are blown;
Supreme on Fame's dread roll thy heroes stand;
All ocean's realms thy naval scepter own;
Of bards, of sages, how august thy band;
And one rich Eden blooms around thy garden'd land.

But O how vast thy crimes! Through heaven's great year
When few centurial suns have trac'd their way,
When southern Europe, worn by feuds severe,
Weak, doating, fallen, has bow'd to Russian sway,
And setting Glory beam'd her farewell ray,
To wastes, perchance, thy brilliant fields shall turn,
In dust thy temples, towers, and towns decay,
The forest howl where London's turrets burn,
And all thy garlands deck thy sad funeral urn.

Some land scarce glimmering in the light of fame,
Scepter'd with arts and arms, if I divine,
Some unknown wild, some shore without a name,
In all thy pomp shall then majestic shine.
As silver-headed Time's slow years decline,
Not ruins only meet th' enquiring eye:
Where round yon mouldering oak vain brambles twine,
The filial stem, already towering high,
Erelong shall stretch his arms and nod in yonder sky.

Where late resounded the wild woodland roar,
Now heaves the palace, now the temple smiles;
Where frown'd the rude rock and the desert shore,
Now pleasure sports, and business want beguiles,
And Commerce wings her flight to thousand isles;
Culture walks forth; gay laugh the loaded fields,
And jocund Labour plays his harmless wiles;
Glad Science brightens, Art her mansion builds,
And Peace uplifts her wand, and Heaven his blessing yields.

O'er these sweet fields, so lovely now and gay,
Where modest Nature finds each want supplied,
Where home-born Happiness delights to play,
And counts her little flock with houshold pride,
Long frown'd, from age to age, a forest wide:
Here hung the slumbering bat; the serpent dire
Nested his brood and drank th' impoison'd tide;
Wolves peal'd the dark, drear nights in hideous choir,
Nor shrunk th' unmeasured howl from Sol's terrific fire.

No charming cot imbank'd the pebbly stream,
No mansion tower'd nor garden teem'd with good,
No lawn expanded to the April beam,
Nor mellow harvest hung its bending load,
Nor science dawn'd, nor life with beauty glow'd,
Nor temple whiten'd in th' enchanting dell:
In clusters wild the sluggish wigwam stood,
And, borne in snaky paths, the Indian fell
Now aim'd the death unseen, now scream'd the tyger-yell.

Even now, perhaps, on human dust I tread,
Pondering with solemn pause the wrecks of time:
Here sleeps, perchance, among the vulgar dead,
Some Chief, the lofty theme of Indian rhyme,
Who lov'd Ambition's cloudy steep to climb,
And smil'd deaths, dangers, rivals to engage;
Who rous'd his followers' souls to deeds sublime,
Kindling to furnace heat vindictive rage,
And soar'd Cæsarean heights, the Phœnix of his age.

In yon small field, that dimly steals from sight
(From yon small field these meditations grow),
Turning the sluggish soil from morn to night,
The plodding hind laborious drives his plough,
Nor dreams a nation sleeps his foot below:
There, undisturbed by the roaring wave,
Releas'd from war and far from deadly foe,
Lies down in endless rest a nation brave,
And trains in tempests born there find a quiet grave.

ANN ELIZA BLEECKER [1752-1783]

One of the few female poets of the revolutionary era, Ann Eliza Bleecker, whose work was published post-humously, is a minor talent of interest mainly because of her unique attempt at cultivating the refined arts in the wilderness of upstate New York. The achievements of such writers, however, are remarkable in the light of the roles of women, and their difficulty in obtaining an education. In addition to these obstacles, Mrs. Bleecker's very abbreviated life must also be considered in any assessment of her poetic efforts.

To Miss Ten Eyck

Dear Kitty, while you rove through sylvan bowers,
Inhaling fragrance from salubrious flowers,
Or view your blushes mantling in the stream,
When Luna gilds it with her amber beam;
The brazen voice of war awakes our fears,
Impearling every damask cheek with tears
   The savage, rushing down the echoing vales,
Frights the poor hind with ill portending yells;
A livid white his consort's cheeks invest;
She drops her blooming infant from her breast;
She tries to fly, but quick recoiling sees
The painted Indian issuing from the trees;
Then life suspensive sinks her on the plain,
Till dire explosions wake her up again.
Oh, horrid sight! her partner is no more;
Pale is his corse, or only tinged with gore;
Her playful babe is dash'd against the stones,
Its scalp torn off, and fractured all its bones.
Where are the dimpling smiles it lately wore?
Ghastly in agony it smiles no more!
Dumb with amaze, and stupefied with grief,
The captured wretch must now attend her chief:
Reluctantly she quits the scene of blood,
When lo! a sudden light illumes the wood;
She turns, and sees the rising fires expand,
And conflagration roll through half the land;
The western flames to orient skies are driven,
And change the azure to a sable heaven.
   Such are our woes, my dear, and be it known
Many still suffer what I tell of one:
No more Albania's sons in slumber lie,
When Cynthia's crescent gleams along the sky;
But every street patrole, and through the night
Their beamy arms reflect a dreadful light.
   Excuse, dear girl, for once this plaintive strain;
I must conclude, lest I transgress again.

DAVID HUMPHREYS [1753-1818]

Another of the Connecticut Wits whose life spanned several careers, Humphreys was a soldier as Washington's aide-de-camp, and a diplomat as minister to Spain and to Portugal, as well as an able poet.

His poems evince great patriotism, and the selection presented here celebrates liberty and democracy.

The Happiness of America, selections [1786]

Thrice happy race! how blest were freedom's heirs,
Blest if they knew what happiness is theirs,
Blest if they knew to them alone 'tis given
To know no sov'reign but the *law* and *Heaven!*
That *law* for them and Albion's realms alone
On sacred justice elevates her throne,
Regards the poor, the fatherless protects,
The widow shields, the proud oppressor checks.
Blest if they knew beneath umbrageous trees
To prize the joys of innocence and ease,
Of peace, of health, of temp'rance, toil, and rest,
And the calm sun-shine of the conscious breast.
For them the spring his annual task resumes,
Invests in verdure and adorns in blooms
Earth's parent lap and all her wanton bow'rs
In foliage fair with aromatic flow'rs.
Their fanning wings the zephyrs gently play,
And winnow blossoms from each floating spray;
In bursting buds the embryo fruits appear,
The hope and glory of the rip'ning year.
The mead that courts the scythe, the pastur'd vale,
And garden'd lawn their breathing sweets exhale;
On balmy winds a cloud of fragrance moves,
And floats the odours of a thousand groves;
For them young summer sheds a brighter day,
Matures the germe with his prolific ray,
With prospects cheers, demands more stubborn toil,
And pays their efforts from the grateful soil:
The lofty maize its ears luxuriant yields,
The yellow harvests gild the laughing fields,
Extend o'er all th' interminable plain,
And wave in grandeur like the boundless main.
For them the flock o'er green savannas feeds,
For them high-prancing bound the playful steeds,
For them the heifers graze sequester'd dales,
Or pour white nectar in the brimming pails.

To them, what time the hoary frosts draw near,
Ripe autumn brings the labours of the year.
To nature's sons how fair th' autumnal even,
The fading landscape and impurpled heaven,
As from their fields they take their homeward way,
And turn to catch the sun's departing ray!
What streaming splendours up the skies are roll'd,
Whose colours beggar Tyrian dyes and gold!
'Till night's dun curtains, wide o'er all display'd,
Shroud shad'wy shapes in melancholy shade.
Then doubling clouds the wintry skies deform,
And, wrapt in vapour, comes the roaring storm,
With snows surcharg'd from tops of mountains sails,
Loads leafless trees and fills the whiten'd vales.
Then desolation strips the faded plains,
Then tyrant death o'er vegetation reigns;
The birds of Heav'n to other climes repair,
And deep'ning glooms invade the turbid air.
Nor then unjoyous winter's rigours come,
But find them happy and content with home:
Their gran'ries fill'd, the task of culture past,
Warm at their fire they hear the howling blast,
With patt'ring rain and snow or driving sleet,
Rave idly loud and at their window beat;
Safe from its rage, regardless of its roar,
In vain the tempest rattles at the door.
The tame brutes shelter'd, and the feather'd brood,
From them, more provident, demand their food:
'Tis then the time from hoarding cribs to feed
The ox laborious and the noble steed;
'Tis then the time to tend the bleating fold,
To strow with litter and to fence from cold.
The cattle fed, the fuel pil'd within,
At setting day the blissful hours begin:
'Tis then, sole owner of his little cot,
The farmer feels his independent lot,
Hears with the crackling blaze that lights the wall
The voice of gladness and of nature call,
Beholds his children play, their mother smile,
And tastes with them the fruit of summer's toil.

PHILLIS WHEATLEY [1753-1784]

Phillis Wheatley holds an extraordinary place in American cultural history: a black, female slave, without formal education, sent to an alien country as a child, she was a published poet at a time when few women could even read and write.

While her poetry is largely derivative and not original, and while her concerns are not with the plight of her own people, her achievements as the first Afro-American female poet are substantial and remarkable.

On Virtue [1773]

O thou bright jewel in my aim I strive
To comprehend thee. Thine own words declare
Wisdom is higher than a fool can reach.
I cease to wonder, and no more attempt
Thine height t'explore, or fathom thy profound.
But, O my soul, sink not into despair,
Virtue is near thee, and with gentle hand
Would now embrace thee, hovers o'er thine head.
Fain would the heav'n-born soul with her converse,
Then seek, then court her for her promis'd bliss.

Auspicious queen, thine heav'nly pinions spread,
And lead celestial *Chastity* along;
Lo! now her sacred retinue descends,
Array'd in glory from the orbs above.
Attend me, *Virtue*, thro' my youthful years!
O leave me not to the false joys of time!
But guide my steps to endless life and bliss.
Greatness, or *Goodness*, say what I shall call thee,
To give an higher appellation still,
Teach me a better strain, a nobler lay,
O Thou, enthron'd with Cherubs in the realms of day!

On Being Brought From Africa To America [1773]

'Twas mercy brought me from my *Pagan* land,
Taught my benighted soul to understand
That there's a God, that there's a *Saviour* too:
Once I redemption neither sought nor knew.
Some view our sable race with scornful eye,
"Their colour is a diabolic die."
Remember, *Christians, Negroes*, black as *Cain*,
May be refin'd, and join th' angelic train.

An Hymn to the Morning [*1773*]

Attend my lays, ye ever honour'd nine,
Assist my labours, and my strains refine;
In smoothest numbers pour the notes along,
For bright *Aurora* now demands my song.

Aurora hail, and all the thousand dies,
Which deck thy progress through the vaulted skies:
The morn awakes, and wide extends her rays,
On ev'ry leaf the gentle zephyr plays;
Harmonious lays the feather'd race resume,
Dart the bright eye, and shake the painted plume.

Ye shady groves, your verdant gloom display
To shield your poet from the burning day:
Calliope awake the sacred lyre,
While thy fair sisters fan the pleasing fire:
The bow'rs, the gales, the variegated skies
In all their pleasures in my bosom rise.

See in the east th' illustrious king of day!
His rising radiance drives the shades away—
But Oh! I feel his fervid beams too strong,
And scarce begun, concludes th' abortive song.

An Hymn to the Evening [*1773*]

Soon as the sun forsook the eastern main
The pealing thunder shook the heav'nly plain;
Majestic grandeur! From the zephyr's wing,
Exhales the incense of the blooming spring.
Soft purl the streams, the birds renew their notes,
And through the air their mingled music floats.

Through all the heav'ns what beauteous dies are spread!
But the west glories in the deepest red:
So may our breasts with ev'ry virtue glow,
The living temples of our God below!

Fill'd with the praise of him who gives the light;
And draws the sable curtains of the night,
Let placid slumbers sooth each weary mind,
At morn to wake more heav'nly, more refin'd;
So shall the labours of the day begin
More pure, more guarded from the snares of sin.

Night's leaden sceptre seals my drowsy eyes,
Then cease, my song, till fair *Aurora* rise.

On Imagination [*1773*]

Thy various works, imperial queen, we see,
How bright their forms! how deck'd with pomp by thee!
Thy wond'rous acts in beauteous order stand,
And all attest how potent is thine hand.

From *Helicon's* refulgent heights attend,
Ye sacred choir, and my attempts befriend:
To tell her glories with a faithful tongue,
Ye blooming graces, triumph in my song.

Now here, now there, the roving *Fancy* flies,
Till some lov'd object strikes her wand'ring eyes,
Whose silken fetters all the senses bind,
And soft captivity involves the mind.

Imagination! who can sing thy force?
Or who describe the swiftness of thy course?
Soaring through air to find the bright abode,

Th' empyreal palace of the thund'ring God,
We on thy pinions can surpass the wind,
And leave the rolling universe behind:
From star to star the mental optics rove,
Measure the skies, and range the realms above.
There in one view we grasp the mighty whole,
Or with new worlds amaze th' unbounded soul.

Though *Winter* frowns to *Fancy's* raptur'd eyes
The fields may flourish, and gay scenes arise;
The frozen deeps may break their iron bands,
And bid their waters murmur o'er the sands.
Fair *Flora* may resume her fragrant reign,
And with her flow'ry riches deck the plain;
Sylvanus may diffuse his honours round,
And all the forest may with leaves be crown'd:
Show'rs may descend, and dews their gems disclose,
And nectar sparkle on the blooming rose.

Such is thy pow'r, nor are thine orders vain,
O thou the leader of the mental train:
In full perfection all thy works are wrought,
And thine the sceptre o'er the realms of thought.
Before thy throne the subject-passions bow,
Of subject-passions sov'reign ruler Thou,
At thy command joy rushes on the heart,
And through the glowing veins the spirits dart.

Fancy might now her silken pinions try
To rise from earth, and sweep th' expanse on high;
From *Tithon's* bed now might *Aurora* rise,
Her cheeks all glowing with celestial dies,
While a pure stream of light o'er flows the skies.
The monarch of the day I might behold,
And all the mountains tipt with radiant gold,
But I reluctant leave the pleasing views,
Which *Fancy* dresses to delight the *Muse;*
Winter austere forbids me to aspire,

And northern tempests damp the rising fire;
They chill the tides of *Fancy's* flowing sea.
Cease then, my song, cease the unequal lay.

To S.M. A Young African Painter, On Seeing His Works

To show the lab'ring bosom's deep intent,
And thought in living characters to paint,
When first thy pencil did those beauties give,
And breathing figures learnt from thee to live,
How did those prospects give my soul delight,
A new creation rushing on my sight?
Still, wond'rous youth! each noble path pursue,
On deathless glories fix thine ardent view;
Still may the painter's and the poet's fire
To aid thy pencil, and thy verse conspire!
And may the charms of each seraphic theme
Conduct thy footsteps to immortal fame!
High to the blissful wonders of the skies
Elate thy soul, and raise thy wishful eyes.
Thrice happy, when exalted to survey
That splendid city, crown'd with endless day,
Whose twice six gates on radiant hinges ring:
Celestial *Salem* blooms in endless spring.

Calm and serene thy moments glide along,
And may the muse inspire each future song!
Still, with the sweets of contemplation bless'd,
May peace with balmy wings your soul invest!
But when these shades of time are chas'd away,
And darkness ends in everlasting day,
On what seraphic pinions shall we move,
And view the landscapes in the realms above?
There shall thy tongue in heav'nly murmurs flow,
And there my muse with heav'nly transport glow:
No more to tell of *Damon's* tender sighs,

Or rising radiance of *Aurora's* eyes,
For nobler themes demand a nobler strain,
And purer language on th' ethereal plain.
Cease, gentle muse! the solemn gloom of night
Now seals the fair creation from my sight.

His Excellency General Washington [*1773*]

Celestial choir! enthron'd in realms of light,
Columbia's scenes of glorious toils I write.
While freedom's cause her anxious breast alarms,
She flashes dreadful in refulgent arms.
See mother earth her offspring's fate bemoan,
And nations gaze at scenes before unknown!
See the bright beams of heaven's revolving light
Involved in sorrows and the veil of night!
  The goddess comes, she moves divinely fair,
Olive and laurel binds her golden hair:
Wherever shines this native of the skies,
Unnumber'd charms and recent graces rise.
Muse! how propitious while my pen relates
How pour her armies through a thousand gates,
As when *Eolus* heaven's fair face deforms,
Enwrapp'd in tempest and a night of storms;
Astonish'd ocean feels the wild uproar,
The refluent surges beat the sounding shore;
Or thick as leaves in Autumn's golden reign,
Such, and so many, moves the warrior's train.
In bright array they seek the work of war,
Where high unfurl'd the ensign waves in air.
Shall I go to Washington their praise recite?
Enough thou know'st them in the fields of fight.
Thee, first in peace and honours,——we demand
The grace and glory of thy martial band.
Fam'd for thy valour, for thy virtues more,

Hear every tongue thy guardian and implore!
    One century scarce perform'd its destined round,
When *Gallic* powers *Columbia's* fury found;
And so may you, whoever dares disgrace
The land of freedom's heaven defended race!
Fir'd are the eyes of nations on the scales,
For in their hopes *Columbia's* arm prevails.
Anon *Britannia* droops the pensive head,
While round increase the rising hills of dead.
Ah! cruel blindness to *Columbia's* state!
Lament thy thirst of boundless power too late.
    Proceed, great chief, with virtue on thy side,
Thy ev'ry action let the goddess guide.
A crown, a mansion, and a throne that shine,
With gold unfading, *Washington!* be thine.

JOEL BARLOW [1754-1812]

One of the most interesting, if not ablest, of the Connecticut Wits, Barlow had, from his time at Yale where he was class poet, aspired to poetic greatness.

He yearned to celebrate America in an epic form which would signal the rise of a national literature. In this quest he wrote "The Vision of Columbus," which was enthusiastically received by his fellow countrymen, hungry for confirmation of their new national spirit and pride. Washington hailed him as "one of the Bards."

In the twenty years following Yale, Barlow's attitudes and beliefs underwent considerable change. His initial conservatism, common to the Connecticut Wits, gave way to radicalism, and he was identified with Thomas Paine and was an ardent supporter of the French Revolution. He subsequently became American minister to France, and died in Poland on a diplomatic mission to Napoleon during the latter's retreat from Moscow.

Barlow's grand poetic ambitions notwithstanding, he is now best remembered for "The Hasty Pudding," a mock epic which he wrote while homesick in France. It still stands as an outstanding piece of light verse.

The Vision of Columbus, selections [*1870-1887*]

From
Book I

Long had the Sage, the first who dar'd to brave
The unknown dangers of the western wave,
Who taught mankind where future empires lay
In these fair confines of descending day,
With cares o'erwhelm'd, in life's distressing gloom,
Wish'd from a thankless world of peaceful tomb;
While kings and nations, envious of his name,
Enjoy'd his labours and usurp'd his fame,
And gave the chief, from promis'd empire hurl'd,
Chains for a crown, a prison for a world.
    Now night and silence held their lonely reign,
The half-orb'd moon declining to the main;
Descending clouds, o'er varying ether driven,
Obscur'd the stars, and shut the eye from heaven;
Cold mists through op'ning grates the cell invade,
And deathlike terrors haunt the midnight shade;
When from a visionary, short repose,
That rais'd new cares and temper'd keener woes,
Columbus woke, and to the walls address'd
The deep-felt sorrows of his manly breast.
    "Here lies the purchase, here the wretched spoil,
Of painful years and persevering toil:
For these dread walks, this hideous haunt of pain,
I trac'd new regions o'er the pathless main,
Dar'd all the dangers of the dreary wave,
Hung o'er its clefts and topp'd the surging grave,
Saw billowy seas in swelling mountains roll,
And bursting thunders rock the reddening pole,
Death rear his front in every dreadful form,
Gape from beneath and blacken in the storm;
Till, tost far onward to the skirts of day,
Where milder suns dispens'd a smiling ray,
Through brighter skies my happier sails descry'd

The golden banks that bound the western tide,
And gave th' admiring world that bounteous shore,
Their wealth to nations and to kings their power.
"Oh land of wonders, dear, delusive coast,
To these fond aged eyes for ever lost!
No more thy flowery vales I travel o'er,
For me thy mountains rear the head no more,
For me thy rocks no sparkling gems unfold,
Or streams luxuriant wear their paths in gold:
From realms of promis'd peace for ever borne,
I hail dread anguish, and in secret mourn.
"But dangers past, a world explor'd in vain,
And foes triumphant shew but half my pain.
Dissembling friends, each earlier joy who gave,
And fir'd my youth the storms of fate to brave,
Swarm'd in the sunshine of my happier days,
Pursu'd the fortune and partook the praise,
Bore in my doubtful cause a two-fold part,
The garb of friendship and the viper's heart,
Now pass my cell with smiles of sour disdain,
Insult my woes and triumph in my pain.
"One gentle guardian Heav'n indulgent gave,
And now that guardian slumbers in the grave.
Hear from above, thou dear, departed Shade!
As once my joys, my present sorrows aid:
Burst my full heart, afford that last relief,
     Breathe back my sighs and reinspire my grief!
Still in my sight thy royal form appears,
Reproves my silence and demands my tears.
On that blest hour my soul delights to dwell
When thy protection bade the canvass swell,
When kings and courtiers found their factions vain,
Blind Superstition shrunk beneath her chain,
The sun's glad beam led on the circling way,
And isles rose beauteous in the western day.
But o'er those silv'ry shores, that new domain,
What crowds of tyrants fix their horrid reign!

Again bold Freedom seeks her kindred skies,
Truth leaves the world, and Isabella dies.
Oh, lend thy friendly shroud to veil my sight,
That these pain'd eyes may dread no more the light!
These welcome shades shall close my instant doom,
And this drear mansion moulder to a tomb."
    Thus mourn'd the hapless man. A thundering sound
Roll'd round the shuddering walls and shook the ground;
O'er all the dome, where solemn arches bend,
The roofs unfold and streams of light descend;
The growing splendor fill'd th' astonish'd room,
And gales etherial breath'd a glad perfume.
Mild in the midst a radiant seraph shone,
Rob'd in the vestments of the rising sun;
Tall rose his stature, youth's primeval grace
Adorn'd his limbs and brighten'd in his face;
His closing wings, in golden plumage drest,
With gentle sweep came folding o'er his breast;
His locks in rolling ringlets glittering hung,
And sounds melodious mov'd his heav'nly tongue.
    "Rise, trembling Chief; to scenes of rapture rise;
This voice awaits thee from th' approving skies.
Thy just complaints, in God's own presence known,
Have call'd compassion from his bounteous throne.
Assume no more the deep desponding strain
Nor count thy toils nor deem thy virtues vain.
Tho' faithless men thy injur'd worth despise,
'Tis thus they treat the blessings of the skies:
For look thro' nature, Heav'n's own conduct trace;
What power divine sustains th' unthankful race!
From that great source, that life-inspiring soul,
Suns drew their light and systems learn'd to roll,
Time walk'd the silent round, and life began,
And God's fair image stamp'd the mind of man;
His cares, his bounties fill the realms of space,
And shine superior in thy favour'd race;
Men speak their wants, th' all-bounteous hand supplies,
And gives the good that mortals dare despise.
In these dark vales where blinded faction sways,
Wealth, pride, and conquest claim the palm of praise,

Aw'd into slaves while grov'ling millions groan
And blood-stain'd steps lead upwards to a throne.
Far other wreaths thy virtuous temples claim,
Far nobler honours build thy sacred name;
Be thine the joys immortal minds that grace,
And thine the toils that bless a kindred race.
   "Now raise thy ravish'd soul to scenes more bright,
The vision'd ages rising on thy sight;
For, wing'd with speed, from worlds of light I came,
To sooth thy grief and show thy distant fame.
As that great Seer whose animating rod
Taught Israel's sons the wonder-working God,
Who led thro' dreary wastes the murm'ring band
To the rich confines of the promis'd land,
Oppress'd with years from Pisgah's beauteous height
O'er boundless regions cast the raptur'd sight,
The bliss of unborn nations warm'd his breast,
Repaid his toils and sooth'd his soul to rest:
Thus o'er thy subject wave shalt thou behold
Far happier realms their future charms unfold,
In nobler pomp another Pisgah rise,
Beneath whose foot thy new-found Canaan lies;
There, rapt in vision, hail the distant clime,
And taste the blessings of remotest time."
   The Seraph spoke; and now before them lay
(The doors unbarr'd) a steep ascending way,
That through disparting shades arose on high,
Reach'd o'er the hills and lengthen'd up the sky,
Show'd a clear summit rich with rising flowers,
That breathe their odours through celestial bowers;
   O'er proud Hispanian spires it looks sublime,
Subjects the Alps and levels all the clime.
Led by the Power, Columbus gain'd the height;
A touch from heav'n sublim'd his mortal sight,
And calm beneath them flow'd the western main,
Far stretch'd, immense, a sky-encircled plain;
No sail, no isle, no cloud invests the bound,
Nor billowy surge disturbs th' unvaried round,

Till deep in distant heav'ns the sun's dim ray
Topp'd unknown cliffs and call'd them up to day.
  Slow glimmering into sight wide regions drew,
And rose and brighten'd on th' expanding view;
Fair sweep the waves, the lessening ocean smiles,
And breathes the fragrance of a thousand isles;
Near and more near the long-drawn coasts arise,
Bays stretch their arms, and mountains life the skies,
The lakes, unfolding, point the streams their way,
The plains, the hills, their spreading skirts display,
The vales draw forth, high walk th' approaching groves,
And all the majesty of nature moves.
  O'er the wild climes his eyes delighted rove,
Where lands extend and glittering waters move;
He saw through central realms the winding shore
Spread the deep Gulph his sail had trac'd before,
The Darien isthmus meet the raging tide,
Join distant lands and neighb'ring seas divide,
On either side the shores unbounded bend,
Push wide their waves and to the poles ascend,
While two great continents united rise,
Broad as the main and lengthen'd with the skies.

From
Book V

Now where the sheeted flames thro' Charlestown roar,
And lashing waves hiss round the burning shore,
Thro' the deep folding fires dread Bunker's height
Thunders o'er all and shows a field of fight.
Like shad'wy phantoms in an evening grove
To the dark strife the closing squadrons move:
They join, they break, they thicken, thro' the air,
And blazing batteries burst along the war;

Now wrapp'd in reddening smoke, now dim in sight,
They sweep the hill or wing the downward flight;
Here, wheel'd and wedg'd, Britannia's veterans turn,
And the long lightnings from their mousquets burn;
There scattering strive the thin colonial train,
And broken squadrons still the field maintain;
Britons in fresh battalions rise the height,
And with increasing vollies give the fight.
Till, smear'd with clouds of dust and bath'd in gore,
As growing foes their rais'd artillery pour,
Columbia's host moves o'er the field afar,
And saves by slow retreat the sad remains of war.
There strides bold Putnam, and from all the plains
Calls the tir'd troops, the tardy rear sustains,
And, mid the whizzing deaths that fill the air,
Waves back his sword and dares the foll'wing war.
    Thro' falling fires Columbus sees remain
Half of each host in heaps promiscuous slain,
While dying crowds the lingering life-blood pour,
And slippery steeps are trod with prints of gore.
There, glorious Warren, thy cold earth was seen;
There spring thy laurels in immortal green:
Dearest of chiefs that ever press'd the plain,
In freedom's cause with early honours slain,
Still dear in death as when in fight you mov'd,
By hosts applauded and by Heav'n approv'd;
The faithful Muse shall tell the world thy fame,
And unborn realms resound th' immortal name.

The Hasty Pudding [*1793*]

A Poem, In Three Cantos

Omne tulit punctum qui miscuit utile dulci.
He makes a good breakfast who mixes pudding with molasses.

Preface

A simplicity in diet, whether is be considered with reference to the happiness of individuals or the prosperity of a nation, is of more consequence than we are apt to imagine. In recommending so important an object to the rational part of mankind, I wish it were in my power to do it in such a manner as would be likely to gain their attention. I am sensible that it is one of those subjects in which example has infinitely more power than the most convincing arguments or the highest charms of poetry. Goldsmith's *Deserted Village*, though possessing these two advantages in a greater degree than any other work of the kind, has not prevented villages in England from being deserted. The apparent interest of the rich individuals, who form the taste as well as the laws in that country, has been against him; and with that interest it has been vain to contend.

The vicious habits which in this little piece I endeavor to combat, seem to me not so difficult to cure. No class of people has any *interest* in supporting them; unless it be the interest which certain families may feel in vying with each other in sumptuous entertainments. There may indeed be some instances of depraved appetites, which no arguments will conquer; but these must be rare. There are very few persons but what would always prefer a plain dish for themselves, and would prefer it likewise for their guests, if there were no risk of reputation in the case. This difficulty can only be removed by example; and the example should proceed from those whose situation enables them to take the lead in forming the manners of a nation. Persons of this description in America, I should hope, are neither above nor below the influence of truth and reason, when conveyed in language suited to the subject.

Whether the manner I have chosen to address my arguments to them be such as to promise any success is what I cannot decide. But I

certainly had hopes of doing some good, or I should not have taken
the pains of putting so many rimes together. The example of domestic
virtues has doubtless a great effect. I only wish to rank *simplicity of
diet* among the virtues. In that case I should hope it will be cherished
and more esteemed by others than it is at present.

The Author

Canto I

Ye Alps audacious, through the heavens that rise,
To cramp the day and hide me from the skies;
Ye Gallic flags, that o'er their heights unfurled,
Bear death to kings, and freedom to the world,
I sing not you. A softer theme I choose,
A virgin theme, unconscious of the muse,
But fruitful, rich, well suited to inspire
The purest frenzy of poetic fire.
    Despise it not, ye bards to terror steeled,
Who hurl your thunders round the epic field;
Nor ye who strain your midnight throats to sing
Joys that the vineyard and the stillhouse bring;
Or on some distant fair your notes employ,
And speak of raptures that you ne'er enjoy.
I sing the sweets I know, the charms I feel,
My morning incense, and my evening meal,
The sweets of Hasty Pudding. Come, dear bowl,
Glide o'er my palate, and inspire my soul.
The milk beside thee, smoking from the kine,
Its substance mingled, married in with thine,
Shall cool and temper thy superior heat,
And save the pains of blowing while I eat.
    Oh! could the smooth, the emblematic song ,
Flow like thy genial juices o'er my tongue,
Could those mild morsels in my numbers chime,
And, as they roll in substance, roll in rime,
No more thy awkward unpoetic name
Should shun the muse, or prejudice thy fame;
But rising grateful to the accustomed ear,

All bards should catch it, and all realms revere!
    Assist me first with pious toil to trace
Through wrecks of time thy lineage and thy race;
Declare what lovely squaw, in days of yore,
(Ere great Columbus sought thy native shore)
First gave thee to the world; her works of fame
Have lived indeed, but lived without a name.
Some tawny Ceres, goddess of her days,
First learned with stones to crack the well-dried maize,
Through the rough sieve to shake the golden shower,
In boiling water stir the yellow flour:
The yellow flour, bestrewed and stirred with haste,
Swells in the flood and thickens to a paste,
Then puffs and wallops, rises to the brim,
Drinks the dry knobs that on the surface swim;
The knobs at last the busy ladle breaks,
And the whole mass its true consistence takes.
    Could but her sacred name, unknown so long,
Rise, like her labors, to the son of song,
To her, to them, I'd consecrate my lays,
And blow her pudding with the breath of praise.
If 'twas Oella whom I sang before,
I here ascribe her one great virtue more.
Not through the rich Peruvian realms alone
The fame of Sol's sweet daughter should be known,
But o'er the world's wide climes should live secure,
Far as his rays extend, as long as they endure.
    Dear Hasty Pudding, what unpromised joy
Expands my heart, to meet thee in Savoy!
Doomed o'er the world through devious paths to roam,
Each clime my country, and each house my home,
My soul is soothed, my cares have found an end,
I greet my long-lost, unforgotten friend.
    For thee through Paris, that corrupted town,
How long in vain I wandered up and down,
Where shameless Bacchus, with his drenching hoard,
Cold from his cave usurps the morning board.
London is lost in smoke and steeped in tea;

No Yankee there can lisp the name of thee;
The uncouth word, a libel on the town,
Would call a proclamation from the crown.
For climes oblique, that fear the sun's full rays,
Chilled in their fogs, exclude the generous maize;
A grain whose rich luxuriant growth requires
Short gentle showers, and bright ethereal fires.
      But here, though distant from our native shore,
With mutual glee we meet and laugh once more.
The same! I know thee by that yellow face,
That strong complexion of true Indian race,
Which time can never change, nor soil impair,
Nor Alpine snows, nor Turkey's morbid air;
For endless years, through every mild domain,
Where grows the maize, there thou art sure to reign.
      But man, more fickle, the bold incense claims,
In different realms to give thee different names.
Thee the soft nations round the warm Levant
polanta call, the French of course *polenta;*
Ev'n in thy native regions, how I blush
To hear the Pennsylvanians call thee *mush!*
On Hudson's banks, while men of Belgic spawn
Insult and eat thee by the name *suppawn.*
All spurious appellations, void of truth;
I've better known thee from my earliest youth,
Thy name is *Hasty Pudding!* thus our sires
Were wont to greet thee fuming from their fires;
And while they argued in thy just defense
With logic clear, they thus explained the sense:
"In *haste* the boiling cauldron, o'er the blaze,
Receives and cooks the ready-powdered maize;
In *haste* 'tis served, and then in equal *haste,*
With cooling milk, we make the sweet repast.
No carving to be done, no knife to grate
The tender ear, and wound the stony plate;
But the smooth spoon, just fitted to the lip,
And taught with art the yielding mass to dip,
By frequent journeys to the bowl well stored,

Performs the hasty honors of the board."
Such is thy name, significant and clear,
A name, a sound to every Yankee dear,
But most to me, whose heart and palate chaste
Preserve my pure hereditary taste.
There are who strive to stamp with disrepute
The luscious food, because it feeds the brute;
In tropes of high-strained wit, while gaudy prigs
Compare thy nursling, man, to pampered pigs;
With sovereign scorn I treat the vulgar jest,
Nor fear to share thy bounties with the beast.
What though the generous cow gives me to quaff
The milk nutritious; am I then a calf?
Or can the genius of the noisy swine,
Though nursed on pudding, thence lay claim to mine?
Sure the sweet song, I fashion to thy praise,
Runs more melodious than the notes they raise.
　　My song resounding in its grateful glee,
No merit claims; I praise myself in thee.
My father loved thee through his length of days;
For thee his fields were shaded o'er with maize;
From thee what health, what vigor he possessed,
Ten sturdy freemen from his loins attest;
Thy constellation ruled my natal morn,
And all my bones were made of Indian corn.
Delicious grain! whatever form it take,
To roast or boil, to smother or to bake,
In every dish 'tis welcome still to me,
But most, my Hasty Pudding, most in thee.
　　Let the green succotash with thee contend,
Let beans and corn their sweetest juices blend,
Let butter drench them in its yellow tide,
And a long slice of bacon grace their side;
Not all the plate, how famed soe'er it be,
Can please my palate like a bowl of thee.
　　Some talk of hoe-cake, fair Virginia's pride,
Rich johnny-cake this mouth has often tried;
Both please me well, their virtues much the same;

Alike their fabric, as allied their fame,
Except in dear New England, where the last
Receives a dash of pumpkin in the paste,
To give it sweetness and improve the taste.
But place them all before me, smoking hot,
The big round dumpling rolling from the pot;
The pudding of the bag, whose quivering breast,
With suet lined, leads on the Yankee feast;
The charlotte brown, within whose crusty sides
A belly soft the pulpy apple hides;
The yellow bread, whose face like amber glows,
And all of Indian that the bakepan knows—
You tempt me not—my favorite greets my eyes,
To that loved bowl my spoon by instinct flies.

Canto II

To mix the food by vicious rules of art,
To kill the stomach and to sink the heart,
To make mankind to social virtue sour,
Cram o'er each dish, and be what they devour;
For this the kitchen muse first framed her book,
Commanding sweat to stream from every cook;
Children no more their antic gambols tried,
And friends to physic wandered why they died.
    No so the Yankee—his abundant feast,
With simples furnished, and with plainness dressed,
A numerous offspring gathers round the board,
And cheers alike the servant and the lord;
Whose well-bought hunger prompts the joyous taste,
And health attends them from the short repast.
    While the full pail rewards the milkmaid's toil,
The mother sees the morning cauldron boil;
To stir the pudding next demands their care,
To spread the table and the bowls prepare;
To feed the children, as their portions cool,
And comb their heads, and send them off to school.

Yet may the simplest dish some rules impart,
For nature scorns not all the aids of art.
Ev'n Hasty Pudding, purest of all food,
May still be bad, indifferent, or good,
As sage experience the short process guides,
Or want of skill, or want of care presides.
Whoe'er would form it on the surest plan,
To rear the child and long sustain the man;
To shield the morals while it mends the size,
And all the powers of every food supplies,
Attend the lessons that the muse shall bring.
Suspend your spoons, and listen while I sing.
But since, O man! thy life and health demand
Not food alone, but labor from thy hand,
First in the field, beneath the sun's strong rays,
Ask of thy mother earth the needful maize;
She loves the race that courts her yielding soil,
And gives her bounties to the sons of toil.
When now the ox, obedient to thy call,
Repays the loan that filled the winter stall,
Pursue his traces o'er the furrowed plain,
And plant in measured hills the golden grain.
But when the tender germ begins to shoot,
And the green spire declares the sprouting root,
Then guard your nursling from each greedy foe,
The insidious worm, the all-devouring crow.
A little ashes, sprinkled round the spire,
Soon steeped in rain, will bid the worm retire;
The feathered robber with his hungry maw
Swift flies the field before your man of straw,
A frightful image, such as schoolboys bring
When met to burn the Pope or hang the King.
Thrice in the season, through each verdant row
Wield the strong plowshare and the faithful hoe;
The faithful hoe, a double task that takes,
To till the summer corn, and roast the winter cakes.

Slow springs the blade, while checked by chilling rains,
Ere yet the sun the seat of Cancer gains;
But when his fiercest fires emblaze the land,
Then start the juices, then the roots expand;
Then, like a column of Corinthian mold,
The stalk struts upward, and the leaves unfold;
The busy branches all the ridges fill,
Entwine their arms, and kiss from hill to hill.
Here cease to vex them, all your cares are done;
Leave the last labors to the parent sun;
Beneath his genial smiles the well-dressed field,
When autumn calls, a plenteous crop shall yield.

Now the strong foliage bears the standards high,
And shoots the tall top-gallants to the sky;
The suckling ears their silky fringes bend,
And pregnant grown, their swelling coats distend;
The loaded stalk, while still the burden grows,
O'erhangs the space that runs between the rows;
High as a hop-field waves the silent grove,
A safe retreat for little thefts of love,
When the pledged roasting-ears invite the maid,
To meet her swain beneath the new-formed shade;
His generous hand unloads the cumbrous hill,
And the green spoils her ready basket fill;
Small compensation for the two-fold bliss,
The promised wedding and the present kiss.

Slight depredations these; but now the moon
Calls from his hollow tree the sly raccoon;
And while by night he bears his prize away,
The bolder squirrel labors through the day.
Both thieves alike, but provident of time,
A virtue rare, that almost hides their crime.
Then let them steal the little stores they can,
And fill their granaries from the toils of man;
We've one advantage where they take no part,
With all their wiles they ne'er have found the art
To boil the Hasty Pudding; here we shine

Superior far to tenants of the pine;
This envied boon to man shall still belong,
Unshared by them in substance or in song.
    At last the closing season browns the plain,
And ripe October gathers in the grain;
Deep loaded carts the spacious corn-house fill,
The sack distended marches to the mill;
The laboring mill beneath the burden groans,
And showers the future pudding from the stones;
Till the glad housewife greets the powdered gold,
And the new crop exterminates the old.

Canto III

    The days grow short; but though the falling sun
To the glad swain proclaims his day's work done,
Night's pleasing shades his various task prolong,
And yield new subjects to my various song.
For now, the corn-house filled, the harvest home,
The invited neighbors to the *husking* come;
A frolic scene, where work, and mirth, and play,
Unite their charms, to chase the hours away.
    Where the huge heap lies centered in the hall,
The lamp suspended from the cheerful wall,
Brown corn-fed nymphs, and strong hard-handed beaux,
Alternate ranged, extend in circling rows,
Assume their seats, the solid mass attack;
The dry husks rustle, and the corncobs crack;
The song, the laugh, alternate notes resound,
And the sweet cider trips in silence round.
    The laws of husking every wight can tell;
And sure no laws he ever keeps so well:
For each red ear a general kiss he gains,
With each smut ear he smuts the luckless swains;
But when to some sweet maid a prize is cast,
Red as her lips, and taper as her waist,
She walks the round, and culls one favored beau,
Who leaps, the luscious tribute to bestow.

Various the sport, as are the wits and brains
Of well-pleased lasses and contending swains;
Till the vast mound of corn is swept away,
And he that gets the last ear wins the day.
Meanwhile the housewife urges all her care,
The well-earned feast to hasten and prepare.
The sifted meal already waits her hand,
The milk is strained, the bowls in order stand,
The fire flames high; and, as a pool (that takes
The headlong stream that o'er the milldam breaks)
Foams, roars, and rages with incessant toils,
So the vexed cauldron rages, roars, and boils.
First with clean salt she seasons well the food,
Then strews the flour, and thickens all the flood.
Long o'er the simmering fire she lets it stand;
To stir it well demands a stronger hand;
The husband takes his turn; and round and round
The ladle flies; at last the toil is crowned;
When to the board the thronging huskers pour,
And take their seats as at the corn before.
I leave them to their feast. There still belong
More copious matters to my faithful song.
For rules there are, though ne'er unfolded yet,
Nice rules and wise, how pudding should be ate.
Some with molasses line the luscious treat,
And mix, like bards, the useful with the sweet.
A wholesome dish, and well deserving praise,
A great resource in those bleak wintry days,
When the chilled earth lies buried deep in snow,
And raging Boreas drives the shivering cow.
Blessed cow! thy praise shall still my notes employ,
Great source of health, the only source of joy;
Mother of Egypt's God—but sure, for me,
Were I to leave my God, I'd worship thee.
How oft thy teats these pious hands have pressed!
How oft thy bounties proved my only feast!
How oft I've fed thee with my favorite grain!
And roared, like thee, to find thy children slain!

Ye swains who know her various worth to prize,
Ah! house her well from winter's angry skies.
Potatoes, pumpkins, should her sadness cheer,
Corn from your crib, and mashes from your beer;
When spring returns she'll well acquaint the loan,
And nurse at once your infants and her own.
Milk then with pudding I should always choose;
To this in future I confine my muse,
Till she in haste some further hints unfold,
Well for the young, nor useless to the old.
First in your bowl the milk abundant take,
Then drop with care along the silver lake
Your flakes of pudding; these at first will hide
Their little bulk beneath the swelling tide;
But when their growing mass no more can sink,
When the soft island looms above the brink,
Then check your hand; you've got the portion's due,
So taught our sires, and what they taught is true.
    There is a choice in spoons. Though small appear
The nice distinction, yet to me 'tis clear.
The deep-bowled Gallic spoon, contrived to scoop
In ample draughts the thin diluted soup,
Performs not well in those substantial things,
Whose mass adhesive to the metal clings;
Where the strong labial muscles must embrace,
The gentle curve, and sweep the hollow space.
With ease to enter and discharge the freight,
A bowl less concave but still more dilate,
Becomes the pudding best. The shape, the size,
A secret rests unknown to vulgar eyes.
Experienced feeders can alone impart
A rule so much above the lore of art.
These tuneful lips that thousand spoons have tried,
With just precision could the point decide,
Though not in song; the muse but poorly shines
In cones, and cubes, and geometric lines;
Yet the true form, as near as she can tell,
Is that small section of a goose-egg shell,

Which in two equal portions shall divide
The distance from the center to the side.
    Fear not to slaver; 'tis no deadly sin.
Like the free Frenchman, from your joyous chin
Suspend the ready napkin; or, like me,
Poise with one hand your bowl upon your knee;
Just in the zenith your wise head project,
Your full spoon, rising in a line direct,
Bold as a bucket, heeds no drops that fall,
The wide-mouthed bowl will surely catch them all.

SARAH WENTWORTH MORTON [1759-1846]

Perhaps the most popular woman writer of her time, Sarah
Wentworth Morton was proclaimed the "American Sappho" by her
admiring public.

The wife of the Attorney General of Massachusetts, Mrs. Morton
was a published novelist (*The Power of Sympathy*, 1789) as well as
poetess. Her writing was confined mostly to the first thirty years of
her life, and she did not produce much poetry thereafter.

The African Chief

See how the black ship cleaves the main,
  High bounding o'er the dark blue wave,
Remurmuring with the groans of pain,
  Deep freighted with the princely slave!

Did all the gods of Afric sleep,
  Forgetful of their guardian love,
When the white tyrants of the deep,
  Betrayed him in the palmy grove.

A chief of Gambia's golden shore,
  Whose arm the band of warriors led,
Or more—the lord of generous power,
  By whom the foodless poor were fed.

Does not the voice of reason cry,
  "Claim the first right that nature gave,
From the red scourge of bondage fly,
  Nor deign to live a burden'd slave."

Has not his suffering offspring clung,
  Desponding round his fetter'd knee;
On his worn shoulder, weeping hung,
  And urged one effort to be free?

His wife by nameless wrongs subdued,
  His bosom's friend to death resign'd;
The flinty path-way drench'd in blood;
  He saw with cold and frenzied mind.

Strong in despair, then sought the plain,
  To heaven was raised his steadfast eye,
Resolved to burst the crushing chain,
  Or 'mid the battle's blast to die.

First of his race, he led the band,
  Guardless of danger, hurling round,
Till by his red avenging hand,
  Full many a despot stain'd the ground.

When erst Messenia's sons oppress'd,
  Flew desperate to the sanguine field,
With iron clothed each injured breast,
  And saw the cruel Spartan yield.

Did not the soul to heaven allied,
  With the proud heart as greatly swell,
As when the Roman Decius died,
  Or when the Grecian victim fell?

Do later deeds quick rapture raise,
  The boon Batavia's William won,
Paoli's time-enduring praise,
  Or the yet greater Washington!

If these exalt thy sacred zeal,
  To hate oppression's mad control,
For bleeding Afric learn to feel,
  Whose chieftain claim'd a kindred soul.

Ah, mourn the last disastrous hour,
  Lift the full eye of bootless grief,
While victory treads the sultry shore,
  And tears from hope the captive chief;

While the hard race of pallid hue,
  Unpractised in the power to feel,
Resign him to the murderous crew,
  The horrors of the quivering wheel.

Let sorrow bathe each blushing cheek,
  Bend piteous o'er the tortured slave,
Whose wrongs compassion cannot speak,
  Whose only refuge was the grave.

RICHARD ALSOP [1761-1815]

Another of the Connecticut Wits, Alsop possessed neither the literary ambition nor the poetic talent of his peers.

A prolific writer and translator (from French and Italian), much of his poetry was not published in his lifetime; his following was limited, albeit enthusiastic.

Verses to the Shearwater—On the Morning After a Storm at Sea

Whence with morn's first blush of light
  Com'st thou thus to greet mine eye,
Whilst the furious storm of night
  Hovers yet around the sky?

On the fiery tossing wave,
  Calmly cradled dost thou sleep,
When the midnight tempests rave,
  Lonely wanderer of the deep?

Or from some rude isle afar,
  Castled 'mid the roaring waste,
With the beams of morning's star,
  On lightning pinion dost thou haste?

In thy mottled plumage drest,
  Light thou skimm'st the ocean o'er,
Sporting round the breaker's crest
  Exulting in the tempest's roar.

O'er the vast-rolling watry way
  While our trembling bark is borne,
And joyful peers the lamp of day,
  Lighting up the brow of morn;

As through yon cloud its struggling beams
  Around a partial lustre shed,
And mark at fits with golden gleams
  The mountain billow's surging head;

Whilst the long lines of foamy white,
  At distance o'er the expanse so blue,
As domes and castles spiring bright,
  Commingling, rise on fancy's view—

From wave to wave swift skimming light,
　　Now near, and now at distance found,
Thy airy form, in ceaseless flight,
　　Cheers the lone dreariness around.

Through the vessel's storm-rent sides,
　　When the rushing billows rave;
And with fierce gigantic strides,
　　Death terrific walks the wave,

Still on hovering pinion near,
　　Thou pursuest thy sportive way;
Still uncheck'd by aught of fear,
　　Calmly seek'st thy finny prey.

Far from earth's remotest trace,
　　What impels thee thus to roam?
What hast thou to mark the place
　　When thou seek'st thy distant home?

Without star or magnet's aid,
　　Thou thy faithful course dost keep;
Sportive still, still undismay'd,
　　Lonely wanderer of the deep!

THEODORE DWIGHT [1764-1846]

Like his more famous brother Timothy, Theodore Dwight was a prominent member of the Connecticut Wits. Theodore wrote most of his verse during the early stages of his life; he later was known principally as a journalist and statesman.

African Distress

"Help! oh, help! thou God of Christians!
    Save a mother from despair!
Cruel white men steal my children!
    God of Christians, hear my prayer!

"From my arms by force they're rended,
    Sailors drag them to the sea;
Yonder ship, at anchor riding,
    Swift will carry them away.

"There my son lies, stripp'd, and bleeding;
    Fast, with thongs, his hands are bound.
See, the tyrants, how they scourge him!
    See his sides a reeking wound

"See his little sister by him;
    Quaking, trembling, how she lies!
Drops of blood her face besprinkle;
    Tears of anguish fill her eyes.

"Now they tear her brother from her;
    Down, below the deck, he's thrown;
Stiff with beating, through fear silent,
    Save a single, death-like, groan."

Hear the little creature begging —
    "Take me, white men, for your own!
Spare, oh, spare my darling brother!
    He's my mother's only son.

"See, upon the shore she's raving:
    Down she falls upon the sands:
Now, she tears her flesh with madness;
    Now, she prays with lifted hands.

"I am young, and strong, and hardy;
　　He's a sick, and feeble boy;
Take me, whip me, chain me, starve me,
　　All my life I'll toil with joy.

"Christians! who's the God you worship?
　　Is he cruel, fierce, or good?
Does he take delight in mercy?
　　Or in spilling human blood?

"Ah, my poor distracted mother!
　　Hear her scream upon the shore."—
Down the savage captain struck her,
　　Lifeless on the vessel's floor.

Up his sails he quickly hoisted,
　　To the ocean bent his way;
Headlong plunged the raving mother,
　　From a high rock, in the sea.

Lines on the Death of Washington

Far, far from hence be satire's aspect rude,
No more let laughter's frolic-face intrude,
But every heart be fill'd with deepest gloom,
Each form be clad with vestments of the tomb.
From Vernon's sacred hill dark sorrows flow,
Spread o'er the land, and shroud the world in wo.
From Mississippi's proud, majestic flood,
To where St. Croix meanders through the wood,
Let business cease, let vain amusements fly,
Let parties mingle, and let faction die,
The realm perform, by warm affection led,
Funeral honors to the mighty dead.
　　Where shall the heart for consolation turn,

Where end its grief, or how forget to mourn?
Beyond these clouds appears no cheering ray,
No morning star proclaims th' approach of day.
Ask hoary Age from whence his sorrows come,
His voice is silent, and his sorrow dumb;
Enquire of Infancy why droops his head,
The prattler lisps—"great Washington is dead."
Why bend yon statesmen o'er their task severe?
Why drops yon chief the unavailing tear?
What sullen grief hangs o'er yon martial band?
What deep distress pervades the extended land?
In sad response sounds from shore to shore—
"Our Friend, our Guide, our Father is no more."
  Let fond remembrance turn his aching sight,
Survey the past, dispel oblivion's night,
By Glory led, pursue the mazy road,
Which leads the traveller to her high abode,
Then view that great, that venerated name,
Inscribed in sunbeams on the roll of Fame.
No lapse of years shall soil the sacred spot,
No future age its memory shall blot;
Millions unborn shall mark its sacred fire,
And latest Time behold it and admire.
  A widow'd country! what protecting form
Shall ope thy pathway through the gathering storm!
What mighty hand thy trembling bark shall guide,
Through Faction's rough and overwhelming tide!
The hour is past—thy Washington no more
Descries, with angel-ken, the peaceful shore.
Freed from the terrors of his awful eye,
No more fell Treason seeks a midnight sky,
But crawling forth, on deadliest mischief bent,
Rears her black front, and toils with cursed intent.
Behold! arranged in long, and black array,
Prepared for conflict, thirsting for their prey,
Our foes advance,—nor force nor danger dread,
Their fears all vanish'd when his spirit fled.
Oft, when our bosoms, fill'd with dire dismay,

Saw mischief gather round our country's way;
When furious Discord seized her flaming brand,
And threatened ruin to our infant land;
When faction's imps sow'd thick the seeds of strife,
And aim'd destruction at the bliss of life;
When war with bloody hand her flag unfurl'd,
And her loud trump alarm'd the western world;
His awful voice bade all contention cease,
At his commands the storms were hush'd to peace.
  But who can speak, what accents can relate,
The solemn scenes which marked the great man's fate!
Ye ancient sages, who so loudly claim
The brightest station on the list of Fame,
At his approach with diffidence retire,
His higher worth acknowledge, and admire.
When keenest anguish rack'd his mighty mind,
And the fond heart the joys of life resign'd,
No guilt, nor terror stretch'd its hard control,
No doubt obscured the sunshine of the soul.
Prepared for death, his calm and steady eye,
Look'd fearless upward to a peaceful sky;
While wondering angels point the airy road,
Which leads the Christian to the house of God.

WILLIAM CLIFFTON [1772-1799]

The son of a Philadelphia quaker, Cliffton suffered from poor health from birth and spent most of his abbreviated life in study and literary pursuits.

Cliffton was a gifted and original satirist and lyricist and would have achieved greater prominence had he lived longer.

To a Robin

From winter so dreary and long,
    Escaped, ah! how welcome the day,
Sweet Bob with his innocent song,
    Is return'd to his favorite spray.

When the voice of the tempest was heard,
    As o'er the bleak mountain it pass'd,
He hied to the thicket, poor bird!
    And shrunk from the pitiless blast.

By the maid of the valley survey'd,
    Did she melt at thy comfortless lot?
Her hand, was it stretch'd to thy aid,
    As thou pick'dst at the door of her cot?

She did; and the wintery wind,
    May it howl not around her green grove;
Be a bosom so gentle and kind,
    Only fann'd by the breathings of love.

She did; and the kiss of her swain,
    With rapture, the deed shall requite,
That gave to my window again
    Poor Bob and his song of delight.

To Fancy

Airy traveller, queen of song,
Sweetest fancy, ever young,
I to thee my soul resign;

Rich or beggar'd, chain'd or free,
Let me live and laugh with thee.

Pride perhaps may knock, and say,
"Rise thou sluggard, come away:"
But can he thy joy impart,
Will he crown my leaping heart?
If I banish hence thy smile
Will he make it worth my while?

Is my lonely pittance past,
Fleeting good too light to last,
Lifts my friend the latch no more,
Fancy, thou canst all restore;
Thou canst, with thy airy shell,
To a palace raise my cell.

At night, while stretch'd on lowly bed,
When tyrant tempest shakes my shed,
And pipes aloud; how bless'd am I,
All cheering nymph, if thou art by,
If thou art by to snatch my soul
Where billows rage and thunders roll.

From cloud, o'er peering mountain's brow
We'll mark the mighty coil below,
While round us innocently play
The lightning's flash, and meteor's ray
And, all so sad, some spectre form
Is heard to moan amid the storm.

With thee to guide my steps I'll creep
In some old haunted nook to sleep,
Lull'd by the dreary night-bird's scream,
That flits along the wizard stream
And there, till morning 'gins appear,
The tales of troubled spirits hear.

Sweet's the dawn's ambiguous light,
Quiet pause 'tween day and night,
When, afar, the mellow horn
Chides the tardy-gaited morn,
And asleep is yet the gale
On sea-beat mount, and river'd vale.

But the morn, though sweet and fair,
Sweeter is when thou art there;
Hymning stars successive fade,
Fairies hurtle through the shade,
Love-lorn flowers I weeping see,
If the scene is touch'd by thee.

When unclouded shines the day,
When my spirits dance and play,
To some sunny bank we'll go
Where the fairest roses blow,
And in gamesome vein prepare
Chaplets for thy spangled hair.

Thus through life with thee I'll glide,
Happy still whate'er betide,
And while plodding sots complain
Of ceaseless toil and slender gain,
Every passing hour shall be
Worth a golden age to me.

Then lead on, delightful power,
Lead, Oh! lead me to thy bower;
I to thee my soul resign,
All my future life be thine.
Rich or beggar'd, chain'd or free,
Let me live and laugh with thee.

ROBERT TREAT PAINE [1773-1811]

Robert Treat Paine was one of the most popular poets of his time. A Bostonian and graduate of Harvard, his reputation far surpassed that of any of his contemporaries, and greatly exceeded his talent.

His poems were derivative, lacked originality, and were devoid of feeling. His great celebrity has been attributed to the great craving for a national poet and the concomitant prevalence of poetic bad taste.

The Ruling Passion, selections [*1797*]

Life is a print-shop, where the eye may trace
A different outline mark'd in every face:
From chiefs who laurels reap in fields of blood,
Down to the hind who tills those fields for food;
From the lorn nymph in cloister'd abbey pent,
Whose friars teach to love and to repent,
To the young captive in the Haram's bower,
Blest for a night, and empress of an hour;
From ink's retailers perch'd in *garret* high,
Cobweb'd around with many a mouldy lie,
Down to the pauper's brat who, luckless wight,
Deep in the *cellar* first receiv'd the light;
All, all impell'd, as various passions move,
To write, to starve, to conquer, or to love!
All join to shift life's versicolor'd scenes,
Priests, poets, fiddlers, courtesans, and queens.
And be it pride or dress or wealth or fame,
The acting principle is ne'er the same;
Each takes a different rout, o'er hill or vale,
The tangled forest or the greensward dale.
　　But they who chiefly crowd the field are those
Who live by fashion—Constables and Beaus.
The first, I ween, are men of high report,
The Law's *staff*-officers, and known at court.
The last, sweet elves, whose rival graces vie
To wield the snuff-box or enact a sigh,
To Fashion's *gossamer* their lives devote,
The frize, the cane, the cravat, and the coat;
In taste unpolish'd, yet in *ton* precise,
They sleep at theatres and wake at dice,
While, like the pilgrim's scrip or soldier's pack,
They carry all their fortune on their back.
　　From Fops we turn to Pedants—deep and dull,

Grave without sense, *o'erflowing yet not full.*
See the lank Book-Worm, pil'd with lumbering lore,
Wrinkled in Latin and in Greek fourscore,
With toil incessant *thumbs* the ancient page,
Now *blots* a hero, now *turns down* a sage.
O'er learning's field with leaden eye he strays,
Mid busts of fame and monuments of praise;
With Gothic foot he treads on *flowers* of taste,
Yet stoops to pick the *pebbles* from the waste.
Profound in trifles, he can tell how short
Were Æsop's legs, how large was Tully's wart;
And scal'd by Gunter, marks with joy absurd
The cut of Homer's cloak and Euclid's beard.
Thus through the weary watch of sleepless night
This learned ploughman plods in piteous plight;
Till the dim taper takes French leave to doze,
And the fat folio tumbles on his toes.

ANONYMOUS

The most popular anti-British ballad, and the one which survives as a skillful example of the genre, is the anonymously authored "Nathan Hale."

Nathan Hale was a captain in the Revolutionary army; in 1776, he went as a spy behind the British lines in New York to obtain information sought by Washington; he was captured, brought before General Howe, and summarily executed.

Nathan Hale [*1776*]

The breezes went steadily through the tall pines,
  A saying "Oh! hu-ush!" a saying "Oh! hu-ush!"
As stilly stole by a bold legion of horse,
  For Hale in the bush, for Hale in the bush.

"Keep still!" said the thrush as she nestled her young,
  In a nest by the road, in a nest by the road;
"For the tyrants are near, and with them appear
  What bodes us no good, what bodes us no good."

The brave captain heard it and thought of his home,
  In a cot by the brook, in a cot by the brook,
With mother and sister and memories dear,
  He so gaily forsook, he so gaily forsook.

Cooling shades of the night were coming apace,
  The tattoo had beat, the tattoo had beat.
The noble one sprang from his dark lurking-place
  To make his retreat, to make his retreat.

He warily trod on the dry rustling leaves,
  As he passed through the wood, as he passed through the wood,
And silently gained his rude launch on the shore,
  As she played with the flood, as she played with the flood.

The guards of the camp, on that dark dreary night,
  Had a murderous will, had a murderous will:
They took him and bore him afar from the shore,
  To a hut on the hill, to a hut on the hill.

No mother was there, nor a friend who could cheer,
  In that little stone cell, in that little stone cell.
But he trusted in love from his Father above;
  In his heart all was well, in his heart all was well.

An ominous owl with his solemn bass voice
   Sat moaning hard by, sat moaning hard by:
"The tyrant's proud minions most gladly rejoice,
   For he must soon die, for he must soon die."

The brave fellow told them, no thing he restrained,
   The cruel gen'ral, the cruel gen'ral;
His errand from camp, of the ends to be gained;
   And said that was all, and said that was all.

They took him and bound him and bore him away,
   Down the hill's grassy side, down the hill's grassy side.
'Twas there the base hirelings, in royal array,
   His cause did deride, his cause did deride.

Five minutes were given, short moments, no more,
   For him to repent, for him to repent.
He prayed for his mother, he asked not another;
   To Heaven he went, to Heaven he went.

The faith of a martyr the tragedy showed,
   As he trod the last stage, as he trod the last stage;
And Britons will shudder at gallant Hale's blood,
   As his words do presage, as his words do presage:

"Thou pale king of terrors, thou life's gloomy foe,
   Go frighten the slave, go frighten the slave;
Tell tyrants to you their allegiance they owe;
   No fears for the brave, no fears for the brave."

BIBLIOGRAPHY

I   HISTORY AND CRITICISM

Brooks, Cleanth, R.W.B. Lewis, and Robert Penn Warren. *American Literature, the Makers and the Making:* Volume I. New York: St. Martin's Press, 1973

Emerson, Everett, editor. *Major Writers of Early American Literature.* Madison: University of Wisconsin Press, 1972

Hubbell, Jay B. *The South in American Literature, 1607-1900.* Durham: Duke University Press, 1954

Pearce, Roy Harvey. *The Continuity of American Poetry.* Princeton: Princeton University Press, 1961

Quinn, Arthur Hobson. *The Literature of the American People.* New York: Appleton-Century-Crofts, 1951

Stauffer, Donald Barlow. *A Short History of American Poetry.* New York: E.P. Dutton, 1974

Trent, William Peterfield, John Erskine, Stuart P. Sherman, and Carl Van Doren, editors. *The Cambridge History of American Literature:* Volume I. New York: The Macmillan Company, 1943

Tyler, Moses Coit. *The Literary History of the American Revolution:* Volume I. New York: Frederick Ungar, 1957

Waggoner, Hyatt H. *American Poets, from the Puritans to the Present.* Boston: Houghton Mifflin, 1968

Wells, Henry W. *The American Way of Poetry.* New York: Columbia University Press, 1943

Williams, Stanley T. *The Beginnings of American Poetry, 1620-1855.* Uppsala, 1951

II   COLLECTIONS

Boynton, Percy H., editor. *American Poetry*. Miami: Granger Books, 1978

Bronson, Walter C., editor. *American Poems (1625-1892)*. Great Neck: Granger Books, 1979

Foerster, Norman, Norman S. Grabo, Russell B. Nye, E. Fred Carlisle, and Robert Falk, editors. *American Prose and Poetry*. Boston: Houghton, Mifflin, 1970

Kettell, Samuel, editor. *Specimens of American Poetry*. 3 volumes. New York: Benjamin Blom, 1967

Meserole, Harrison T., Walter Sutton, and Brom Weber, editors. *American Literature, Tradition and Innovation:* Volume I. Lexington: D.C. Heath, 1969

Prescott, Frederick & Gerald D. Sanders, editors. *An Introduction to American Poetry*. Miami: Granger Books, 1976

INDEX

INDEX

INDEX